T0304422

HISTORYHIT

GUIDE TO

Medieval England

HISTORYHIT GUIDE TO

Medieval England

From the Vikings to the Tudors –
and Everything in Between

Matthew Lewis

Introduction by Dan Snow

HODDER &
STOUGHTON

First published in Great Britain in 2024
by Hodder & Stoughton Limited
An Hachette UK company

1

A CIP catalogue record for this title is available
from the British Library

Hardback ISBN 9781399726139
ebook ISBN 9781399726146

Typeset in Adobe Garamond by Goldust Design
Printed and bound in Great Britain by Clays Ltd, Elcograf S.p.A.

Hodder & Stoughton policy is to use papers that are
natural, renewable and recyclable products and made from
wood grown in sustainable forests. The logging and manufacturing
processes are expected to conform to the environmental
regulations of the country of origin.

Hodder & Stoughton Limited
Carmelite House
50 Victoria Embankment
London EC4Y 0DZ

www.hodder.co.uk

Contents

Introduction

E ngland is medieval. When the Roman army left these shores and the Irish, Picts, Saxons, Jutes and Frisians fought over the corpse of Britannia, neither the word nor the idea of England existed. There was warm beer, thankfully, although I fear that orderly queuing and a sense of fair play were still some years in the future. As was Parliament and the English language. There was no Westminster, no football, no monarchy, no cross of St George. England was forged in the centuries that followed that original, apocalyptic Brexit in the Middle Ages: the medieval period. At the end of this period, which we are going to roughly define as the end of the 15th century, around 500 years ago, not only England, but Scotland, Wales and Ireland were recognisable to our modern eye, Christianity had seen off paganism, Oxford and Cambridge were seats of learning, London was the principal city, and English-speaking kings ruled over a well-established realm from their base in Westminster. Chaucer and others had established the English literary tradition, Shakespeare's birth was in the offing. It was all starting to look very familiar.

England as an independent, distinct kingdom did not outlast the medieval world by that long. Within a century or so monarchs ruled jointly over both England and Scotland; within two centuries, in 1707, they formally merged to form Great Britain. So the Kingdom of England was very largely a medieval phenomenon.

This phenomenon has proved so intriguing to the generations

that have followed. The architecture, ideas, stories and fashion of medieval England continue to grip us today. From buildings seeking to boost their magnificence with crenellations and mullioned windows, to fans at the World Cup dressing as medieval knights; we love the *Game of Thrones* franchise, so obviously inspired by the 15th-century Wars of the Roses, with added dragons and Mongols, and video games set in the medieval world; and millions of us enjoy days out at heritage sites featuring catapults, weaving, shield-making and jousting. There is an enduring fascination with Arthur, Alfred, castles, cathedrals, crusades, Vikings, Richard III and his nephews, and English victories against the odds on the bloody fields of that eternal frenemy, France.

When I started History Hit I assumed we would be spending a lot of time and attention on the World Wars and the Tudors. In fact, our audience in Britain and around the world have outed themselves as massive fans of medieval history. Time and again tales of castles and the Black Death, or the stories of everyday medieval lives, top our charts of what people are listening to or watching on our platforms.

That has given me a wonderful opportunity to explore the period. I have helped out as metal detectorists sought to locate a lost medieval battlefield, Brunanburh, a crucible of England itself, where Æthelstan smashed a coalition of British, Irish and Viking enemies who were trying to strangle England at its birth. I have crept through church crypts and along exposed battlements. One highlight was crawling through the tunnels beneath Dover Castle. You can see the marks made by the miners who hacked out the chalk during the terrible siege of 1216, the French attackers and the English defenders both burrowing away deep underground. I have been lucky enough to get close up to original copies of Magna Carta, the rolls of fines from the reign of Henry III, and the shocking mortality records from the Black Death.

The medieval is as fascinating as it is important. Our knowledge is patchy and incomplete, which is why many love it. There is space for conjecture and imagination. Some of the history is familiar. There are warring families and conflict among royal princes. There is ambition, conquest, pandemics, outbreaks of the dancing plague – which saw people dance until they dropped – and scientific breakthrough. But there is also much that is obscure: the worldviews, the superstitions, the religious beliefs and the long-dead, oddly shaped countries. This book is here to help.

History Hit's in-house medieval scholar and Richard III apologist, Matthew Lewis, has conducted hundreds of interviews while making podcasts and TV shows with the world's best medievalists to add to his own encyclopaedic knowledge. He has given us a brilliant primer, an accessible account of nearly a millennium of history that will set out the landscape for anyone who wants to delve deeper. If you want to know your Plantagenets from your Valois, your Edwards from your Henrys, this is the book for you.

Dan Snow, 2024

Chapter 1

The Bit Before 1066, Which Matters Just as Much

Viking raiders attack England : the Great Heathen Army arrives :
the Heptarchy collapses : Alfred of Wessex resists the Vikings :
Æthelstan and the birth of England : Cnut the Great conquers
England : the Anglo-Saxon revival : claimants on Edward the
Confessor's death : Harald Hardrada invades : the Norman
Conquest : Hereward the Wake resists the Normans

From the late 8th century, England was the target of attacks by Scandinavian raiders remembered as the Vikings. The most famous early encounter with the Vikings came on the Holy Island of Lindisfarne off the coast of Northumbria in 793. Sightings and encounters were recorded just before this, the first appearing in 787, but the brutal assault on Holy Island and its community of monks rocked the Christian world. To the pagan Vikings, the monastery was an unguarded store of treasure almost begging to be taken. The monks were unarmed nuisances, but any survivors had value as slaves. The terrifying attack on Lindisfarne is often used to date the beginning of the Viking Age.

Over the decades that followed, Viking raiding parties would return again and again to plunder England's seemingly endless wealth. In 865, a large Viking invasion was dubbed the 'Great Heathen Army' by the Anglo-Saxon Chronicle. This time, their purpose was conquest. The rich, fertile land had proven easy to raid. If they could take it, there would be no more need for long

WHAT WAS A VIKING?

The word 'Viking' is a label applied to Scandinavian people who migrated across Europe from the 8th to the 11th centuries. The word only refers to men, and in a basic translation it means 'pirate' or 'raider' in Old Norse. But Scandinavian people at this time were not all pirates or raiders. There was also no Viking ethnic group or one unified 'Viking' kingdom or Empire.

KINGDOMS OF
THE ANGLO-SAXON
HEPTARCHY

ENGLISH MILES

0   10   20   40   60   80

STRATHCLYDE

NORTHUMBRIA

MERCIA

EAST
ANGLIA

NORTH
WALES

ESSEX

WESSEX

KENT

SUSSEX

BURGHS AND BURYS OF ENGLAND

The suffixes 'burgh', 'borough' and 'bury', all hailing from the early medieval period, mean 'fortified'. Thus Canterbury, Peterborough and Bamburgh all have medieval or earlier fortifications. The Roman equivalent of this is 'caster' or 'chester', referring to a Roman castrum (fort). For example, Winchester or Lancaster.

sea voyages and violent pillaging. They could hang up their axes and enjoy the easy life.

The Great Heathen Army swiftly overran the north and east of England. The army overwintered rather than return home, and would remain in England for 14 years.

By 871, only Wessex remained unconquered. Its new king, Alfred, had bribed the Vikings to leave his realm after a defeat at the Battle of Wilton. Raids into Wessex continued and, in January 878, Chippenham was attacked while the king was staying in the town. He escaped, later establishing a fortress at Athelney, an island in the marshes of Somerset. From there he organised resistance to the Viking invaders.

King Alfred's Resistance

In May 878, Alfred mustered his kingdom and fought the Vikings at the Battle of Edington in Wiltshire. After winning a stunning victory, Alfred pursued the Vikings to Chippenham, laying siege to the town until their supplies ran out. Upon the Viking surrender, Alfred agreed to terms requiring the Viking leader, Guthrum, to convert to Christianity. The independence of Wessex was preserved, and part of the midlands realm of

Mercia would remain under Saxon rule. Guthrum would withdraw beyond a new boundary that ran from the River Thames to the River Lea, on to the River Ouse, and then followed the old Roman road of Watling Street, which is today the A5. It effectively cut England in two, with Anglo-Saxons, dominated by Alfred in Wessex, controlling the south and west, and Vikings ruling the east and north. The area under Viking control became known as the Danelaw – where Danish law prevailed.

Alfred would earn the epithet 'the Great' for his resistance to the seemingly unstoppable Vikings. Another Viking invasion arrived in the early 890s, but Alfred pushed them back until they abandoned their efforts in 896. The king, supported by his son Edward the Elder and his daughter Æthelflæd, Lady of the Mercians, maintained Anglo-Saxon control of part of England. He took the title King of the Anglo-Saxons and created a network of burhs, fortified towns that allowed the local population to shelter within from raids and work together as a defensive unit.

This strategy of organised, coordinated resistance proved successful and Alfred, who died in 899, became a legend in English history. The Vikings, however, began to settle in the Danelaw. A century of tense peace was shattered by the arrival of a new Danish army seeking to exploit the wealth of England.

In 978, Alfred's great-great-grandson Æthelred became King of the English. That title had first been adopted by Alfred's grandson Æthelstan in 927, to signify his rule over all those who spoke the English language. Æthelstan had unified Britain with astonishing success, though his achievements had begun to unravel after his death. Æthelred is known as the Unready, though his nickname in Old English was actually Æthelred Unræd. Unræd meant ill-advised and was a play on Æthelred, which

LISTEN TO THE
PODCAST

The Danelaw

THE ANGLO-SAXONS
AND THE DANELAW

ANGLO-SAXON STATES
THE DANELAW TERRITORIES

ENGLISH NORTHUMBRIA

DANISH NORTHUMBRIA

DANISH MERCIA

THE DANELAW

ENGLISH MERCIA

KINGDOM OF GUTHRUM

WESSEX AND ITS DEPENDENCIES

meant well-advised. So Well-advised the Ill-advised. Maybe it was funnier in the 10th century.

LISTEN TO THE
PODCAST

The Battle of Maldon

From 980 onwards, Danish fleets renewed their raiding on the English coast from Hampshire to Cornwall as well as in Cheshire. In 991, Danes invaded the south-east and defeated Byrhtnoth, Ealdorman of Essex at the Battle of Maldon, a moment immortalised in the poem in Old English named after the battle.

Æthelred's response was to fall back on a previous tactic. He paid the Danes a large sum of money, 3,300 kg of silver, to go away. It worked for a time but only served to convince the Danes that England had vast reserves of wealth that they could get their hands on.

The Danish Conquest

King Sweyn Forkbeard of Denmark led an assault on London in 994 and was bought off. In 1001, Æthelred made another huge payment to buy off raids on the south coast of Devon. The payments became known as Danegeld and are seen as a failure of Æthelred's government, though the tactic had been used before both in England and in France. Æthelred did try other things to counter the threat. In 1002, he did two things that proved important. He married Emma, the daughter of the Duke of Normandy. The foreign match was unusual for an Anglo-Saxon king but proved important to the story of England. In the same year, Æthelred also turned the Vikings' violent tactics against them, ordering the St Brice's Day Massacre. Both sides were capable of shocking acts of violence against leaders and the populace.

On 13 November 1002, all Danish men who could be found in England were slaughtered. Among the dead was reported to be Gunhilde, the sister of Sweyn Forkbeard, and her husband. Vengeance for this, as well as for his countrymen, probably motivated Sweyn's attacks on England from 1002 to 1005, 1006 to 1007, and again from 1009 to 1012. Sweyn was accompanied by Thorkell the Tall, a prominent warlord. When Sweyn returned in 1013, Æthelred had adopted another new tactic. He had hired Thorkell and his men as mercenaries to defend England from Sweyn.

Sweyn proved too strong this time for Æthelred, even with Thorkell's support. Æthelred was driven from England, and Sweyn was proclaimed king. It was short-lived. He ruled for just five weeks before he died. With the Danish claim to the throne of England forged in conquest, Sweyn's son Cnut, on his father's death, failed to obtain recognition as the new king. Instead, Æthelred was invited by the Witenagemot or Witan, England's council of nobles, to return from exile in Normandy, and ruled until his death in 1016. He was succeeded by his son Edmund, known as Ironside because he spent so much of his young life at war. Edmund Ironside became king in April 1013 but died in November the same year.

When Edmund died, Cnut was in England pressing his claim to his father's Crown. He capitalised on Edmund's unexpected passing and snatched power, marrying Æthelred's widow, Emma of Normandy, despite being already married. Cnut would rule England for almost 20 years, until his death in 1035. As King of Denmark and of Norway, he presided over an Anglo-Scandinavian 'North Sea Empire', following Alfred in gaining the epithet 'the Great.'

On his death, there was another power struggle. Cnut's son, Harald Harefoot, sought the Crown but could only attain the position of regent for his half-brother, Emma's son, Harthacnut, who was in Norway. Eventually, when Harthacnut failed to arrive in England, Harald managed to have himself crowned king. In the aftermath of this, Emma's two sons from her marriage to Æthelred returned from exile in Normandy to England.

A letter exists that appears to be from Emma, calling on one of her sons to come and stake a claim to England. We know something about Emma and how she hoped to be remembered because she commissioned her own biography, the *Encomium Emmæ Reginae*. Both her sons would cross the Channel separately. Edward arrived safely, but his brother Alfred fell into the hands of Godwin, Earl of Wessex, an adviser of King Harald. Godwin had the young man blinded, and he soon died from the wounds. Edward fled back to Normandy.

Harald Harefoot died in March 1040, just as Harthacnut was preparing to invade. With his path unexpectedly cleared, Harthacnut was proclaimed king. The new king's health seems to have been a concern, and his mother, Emma, convinced him to invite his half-brother Edward back to England again and recognise him as heir to the throne. Harthacnut agreed, with some sources suggesting they worked together as co-kings until Harthacnut's death in June 1042. Edward became king aged almost 40. Despite his later reputation as a saint and his epithet of the Confessor, Edward could be ruthless. He deprived his mother of all her lands and influence because he blamed her for his life as a penniless exile in Normandy. His 24-year rule would end with his death in 1066, a year that was to change the kingdom of England radically and permanently.

The Norman Conquest

Æthelred and Emma's marriage became more significant in 1066. Emma had crafted for herself an incredible position in England. Æthelred had been significantly older than her, and during his reign she had held little authority. When Cnut became king, and forcibly married Emma, she was the older and more experienced partner, and her influence grew. Emma became Queen of England in 1002 and remained consort for over 30 years. To Cnut, she was a connection to England and a strand of legitimacy for his kingship. To Æthelred, she had been an attempt to stop the Viking threat.

Normandy was, in some ways, a French equivalent to the Danelaw in England. In the early 10th century, the part of Europe known today as France was called West Francia and was the western third of Charlemagne's Frankish empire, which had been broken up among his grandsons. Charles the Great, known as Charlemagne, had ruled a vast European empire from 800 to 814 comprised of West Francia, Middle Francia and East Francia. Those living in the realms were collectively known as the Franks, a name that became synonymous with Christian Europeans and is the root of the name of France and the French. Like England, the Frankish lands were viewed by Viking raiders as rich, easy pickings.

As in England during the 9th century, the Vikings were a menace in northern France. They besieged Paris repeatedly, taking large ransoms in 845 and 885. One Viking leader, named Rollo, besieged Chartres in 911. While he was unsuccessful, the King of West Frankia, Charles the Simple, granted him a parcel of land north of the River Seine, which was expanded in 924 and again in 933. Rollo became Count of Rouen, and in return he converted to Christianity and swore to protect the Seine from other Viking attacks. Although he was not initially referred to as Duke of Normandy, Rollo's establishment of a buffer zone between the Franks and Vikings marked the foundation of Normandy. The name refers to its possession by the North Men, the Normans.

In 1002, Æthelred had sought to marry Emma of Normandy to end Norman support for Viking incursions into England. Emma

THE THREE CONTENDERS FOR THE ENGLISH THRONE IN 1066

Harold Godwinson, Earl of Wessex: brother-in-law of Edward the Confessor and most powerful man in England.

Harald Hardrada, King of Norway: with a distant link to Cnut. Probably the most famous warrior in Europe.

William of Normandy, Duke of Normandy: first cousin once removed of Edward the Confessor and great-nephew of Emma of Normandy. Had secured his power over Normandy by 1060 after a long struggle.

was the great-granddaughter of Rollo. Her Norman connection provided a safe haven for her family when Æthelred was deposed and for her sons after his death. Edward the Confessor had also spent more than 20 years in exile at the Norman court from his early teens, making it likely that his outlook was far more Norman than English when he became King of England in 1042. Emma had created a link between England and Normandy that would endure for centuries.

Edward died childless on 5 January 1066. He had been married for over 20 years. His failure to have an heir added to later views of him as unworldly, holy and saintly. His wife was Edith of Wessex, daughter of Earl Godwin – the same Godwin who had blinded and killed Edward's brother. That must have made their relationship awkward. There were three contenders to succeed Edward the Confessor, and no clear rule as to who held the best claim.

Succession in England did not yet rely on the passing of the Crown to the oldest son. The council, or Witan, had a role in electing the next monarch. Succession might pass to a brother or uncle of a deceased king to avoid a young king, or if the oldest son was considered in some way unsuitable. Between the death of one king and the coronation of another, there was an inter-regnum; there was no king, and that meant no king's peace to be maintained. It could be a dangerous and lawless period, and made a swift coronation desirable.

King Harold Godwinson

Who was next was resolved quickly. Edward the Confessor was buried in Westminster Abbey the day after his death, 6 January. The abbey had been Edward's great foundation. Immediately after the funeral, Edward's brother-in-law, Harold Godwinson, was crowned King Harold II. He claimed that, on his deathbed, Edward had entrusted the kingdom to Harold's care, effectively appointing him heir. The Witan were quick to accept Harold, who was popular and powerful. The matter seemed settled.

The first threat Harold faced came a few months later in May. Harold's brother Tostig had been deposed as Earl of Northumbria in 1065, and Harold had supported King Edward in throwing him out of England. Now, Tostig wanted revenge on his brother. He harried the south coast from the Isle of Wight, but Harold raised an army and sent a fleet to sea, and Tostig was chased away. But if Harold thought that was the end of his troubles that year he was sorely mistaken.

Tostig made his way to the court of Harald Hardrada (Hard Ruler), King of Norway. Harald was a legend in his own lifetime. Exiled from Norway, he had taken refuge with the Kievan Rus', themselves descendants of Vikings, and served in the Byzantine Emperor's personal bodyguard – the Varangian Guard. Here, Harald had taken part in military campaigns around the Mediterranean, grown rich and built a remarkable reputation. By 1046, he had returned to Scandinavia, and by the end of that year he was King of Norway.

In 1066, Harald was about 50 years old and had been King of Norway for 20 years. As with the other contenders, his claim to the throne of England was tenuous. It was claimed that Cnut's son, Harthacnut, had made an agreement with Harald's predecessor Magnus I. If either died childless, the other would succeed them. As Magnus's heir, Harald seized upon the idea of rebuilding Cnut's North Sea Empire. In September 1066, Harald's fleet met up with Tostig's, and they landed in the northeast of England, where Vikings had always enjoyed great success.

The first to react were two brothers. Edwin, Earl of Mercia joined forces with Morcar, who had replaced Tostig as Earl of Northumbria, at York. On 20 September, Edwin and Morcar's armies engaged with those of Harald and Tostig at the Battle of Fulford, two miles south of York. It was a crushing defeat for the English, though the brothers escaped. This would prove to be the last time a Scandinavian army would be victorious on English soil. The loss of English soldiers would also prove decisive later in the year.

In the immediate aftermath, York surrendered to Harald. Tostig must have thought he had tied his fortunes to an unstoppable force, the next King Harald of England. But within days, his brother, King Harold Godwinson, had arrived in the north with a fresh Anglo-Saxon army. He pushed straight through York to find Harald and Tostig at Stamford Bridge, five miles east of the city. On 25 September 1066, the Battle of Stamford Bridge saw the Crown of England disputed on the battlefield.

Caught by surprise, the Norwegian forces were unprepared. The Anglo-Saxon Chronicle explains that one Norwegian warrior blocked the bridge over the river, single-handedly slaying 40 Englishmen and slowing their approach. He was only removed when someone trudged into the river and thrust a spear up from beneath him. The English then crashed into the Norwegian army, and bitter fighting lasted for several hours. Eventually, Harold managed to breach the Norwegian shield wall and outflank his enemy. Harald Hardrada was killed by an arrow in his throat, and Tostig was also slain. The Norwegian army began to fragment, leaderless and without purpose. It was a slaughter. Three hundred ships had brought the invading army. Only 24 were required to take the survivors home. The Battle of Stamford Bridge is a moment often used to mark the end of the Viking Age in England, as the kingdom was never seriously threatened by Scandinavians after this point.

Harold's stunning victory had preserved his Crown, but then came troubling news. Another rival claimant to the throne of England had landed at Pevensey on the south coast on 28 September. Harold hurried south, pausing in London for a week to replenish his forces and formulate a plan. Facing one invasion in the autumn, out of campaigning season, had been a surprise. A second was an unwelcome shock.

William, Duke of Normandy had a claim every bit as tenuous as Harald Hardrada's and indeed as Harold Godwinson's. Known as William the Bastard, he was an illegitimate son of Robert I, the Magnificent, Duke of Normandy and his mistress Herleva. A direct descendant of Rollo the Viking, he was also the great-nephew of Emma of Normandy. This fairly distant blood relation to Edward the Confessor gave William a thin thread by which to claim the throne. He strengthened it by reference to oaths given to him. William claimed Edward had promised to designate him as heir to the throne, though that position was not entirely in Edward's gift. The Witan had a role to play too. Furthermore, William insisted that Harold had been in Normandy as his guest for a time, during which he had sworn an oath on holy relics to support William's claim when the time came. The scene would be immortalised in the Bayeux Tapestry, and the idea of Harold as an oath-breaker was a central part of William's propaganda effort around his invasion. He would claim the Pope's backing for his bid to depose a man who had broken a sacred promise.

The duke had been preparing to cross the Channel for weeks, but bad weather kept him in port. When he did risk it, he was driven back by fierce winds. The omens were poor. Eventually, late in September, William took his chance as storms subsided and sailed across the sea. The Normans made their way from Pevensey to Hastings, erecting wooden castles to help embed themselves and defend their positions. They also harried the countryside. The Bayeux Tapestry shows homes being burned as women and children flee. The tactic was meant to demoralise the population, demonstrate Harold's inability to protect them and goad the ungodly king into leaving the safety of London. Harold's mother and siblings counselled him to wait, rebuild his forces and be ready before he faced William. Enraged and embarrassed by the treatment of his people and confident after his victory against Hardrada, Harold ignored them and marched south.

The Battle of Hastings

On 14 October, the two forces met for a moment that would define the course of English history from that day forward: the Battle of Hastings. Harold rushed south. William's scouts spotted the approaching force and the duke began to march north. Harold hoped to rely on the surprise of his speedy arrival, as he had done at Stamford Bridge, but William was able to remove at least some of that advantage. The armies met at Senlac Hill, a location ideal for neither of them. William was at the bottom of the hill facing the prospect of fighting an enemy on higher ground. Harold was crammed into a narrow spot that prevented him from deploying his forces as he might have hoped.

William knew he had to get Harold off the hill. He launched volleys of arrows, but the shield wall was unmoved. He sent infantry and cavalry up the hill to try to smash through, but the discipline of the Anglo-Saxons held. Eventually, the Normans fled. The Saxons took heart and charged down the hill to rout the enemy. Sources vary as to whether the retreat was genuine or a trick. Either way, the shield wall that had held all day was broken, not by Norman force but by English excitement. The Normans turned, either springing their trap or recognising the opportunity, and encircled the English force. Brutal fighting continued. Harold's brothers Gyrth and Leofwine were killed, but the battle really turned on one moment.

LISTEN TO THE
PODCAST

The Battle
of Hastings

King Harold was killed. Although stories sprang up that he was hit in the eye by an arrow, there is considerable doubt as to whether that was true. The depiction in the Bayeux Tapestry of a figure clutching an arrow embedded in his eye is not definitely Harold and was altered centuries after the Tapestry was created. He seems originally to have been holding a spear. The *Carmen de Hastingae Proelio*, a near-contemporary poem about the battle, tells of a Norman hit squad, which included William himself, punching through the English lines and targeting Harold. William knew the only way to end the fight and claim the Crown was to kill Harold, who was hacked down by this elite squad that had his death as their sole purpose.

The English now fled. The Battle of Hastings had been won by Duke William of Normandy, who now expected to be recognised as the new King of England. The Witan, however, had other ideas. They would not hand the kingdom to this invader so easily. Within days of the battle, the Witan elected Edgar Ætheling as their new monarch. Edgar was about 14 years old, his youth a signal of Anglo-Saxon England's desperation. Edgar was the grandson of Edmund Ironside. His appointment was the final death throe of Anglo-Saxon England. Edgar would never be crowned and would go on to lead an extraordinary life as a rebel and a crusader, but William had not come so far and achieved so much to relinquish the Crown to a boy.

William marched to Dover, then Canterbury, before reaching the south end of London Bridge. London resisted in what would become the last stand of Anglo-Saxon England. William moved west to cross the River Thames at Wallingford, and the mood in England turned. At Berkhamsted, northwest of London, the members of the Witan came before William and submitted to him, recognising the Duke of Normandy as the new King of England.

On Christmas Day 1066, William, later known as the Conqueror, was crowned at Edward the Confessor's Westminster Abbey. The day went horribly wrong. As Norman and Anglo-Saxon voices competed to acclaim William, his soldiers outside mistook the clamour for an uprising. They set fire to buildings around the abbey and the building filled with smoke. Much of the congregation fled. William, reportedly shaking, ordered the clergy to remain and complete his coronation. It was hardly an auspicious start to Norman rule. The Anglo-Saxon elite were swept away and replaced by new Norman overlords. The structures of society were slower to be dismantled as William took control and familiarised himself with his new, exalted position as a king, chosen and anointed by God. Although the Normans were descendants of Vikings, they were firmly French now. England's ties to Scandinavia, which had frequently been fraught but nevertheless formed part of its national identity, were permanently severed, though its new rulers were of Viking heritage. Anglo-Saxon culture and identity would be consumed by customs, systems of government, and not least by a new language of power, which were all French.

Anglo-Saxon England did not therefore die overnight in the wake of Hastings, but it went into terminal decline. Edgar

NORMANDY AND ENGLAND

DURHAM

ENGLAND

LONDON

•WELLS

NORMANDY

FRANCE

Ætheling may have been involved in a failed uprising led by the brothers, Edwin and Morcar, who had lost at Fulford. He then managed to reach the court of King Malcolm III of Scotland, who backed an attempt to take William's throne. The revolt led to the Harrying of the North, when William laid waste to a vast area of the north of England in vengeance for their disobedience. When William made peace with Scotland in 1072, one of the terms was the expulsion of Edgar, who moved to Flanders. On William's death, Edgar became embroiled in the succession crisis that broke out between his sons. In 1097, he invaded Scotland and helped install his nephew, another Edgar, as king there. He then went on to take part in the First Crusade, and was still alive in 1125. After this final mention of him, his fate and date of death are unknown.

Hereward's Rebellion

Resistance to Norman rule was also embodied by a figure remembered as Hereward the Wake, though his epithet may have been a later attempt by the Wake family to associate themselves with his legend. His story is shrouded in myth, but a rebel named Hereward is widely reported as taking up residence on the Isle of Ely, then at the centre of a treacherous swamp. Hereward had been in exile in 1066, but around 1068 returned to England. He found his father dead and his brother murdered by Normans who had snatched his ancestral home. In a rage, he killed them all. After crossing to Flanders to gather support, Hereward came back to England to lead resistance to William. He managed to defeat and outwit the Normans at every turn, infuriating but also impressing William.

Hereward sneaked off the Isle of Ely and went into the Norman court disguised as a potter. He overheard a conversation with a woman about the next plan to attack Ely and committed it to memory before heading into the royal kitchens. When those in the kitchen pushed and shoved him, he reacted violently, killing one soldier and knocking out others. He was chased into the night but escaped. When the attack came on Ely, it was, as Hereward had overheard, led by a witch. She stood atop a wooden tower and muttered a vicious curse on those on the Isle. As she completed the ritual, Hereward and his men sprang from the marshes and set fire to the reeds and the wooden tower. The witch fell and broke her neck as the Normans fled in panic. William was furious.

Shortly after, Hereward offered to appear before William to negotiate peace terms. While in the king's presence, he impressed William with the organisation of his men. The furious Norman barons arranged for a huge man named Ogger to fight Hereward. Hereward won the contest but was arrested for committing violence at the king's court. He was placed in custody but eventually escaped, sending word to William that he would still make peace with the king. William accepted the offer, still impressed by Hereward, and returned his father's lands to him.

Hereward, like Edgar, managed to rebel against William the Conqueror, a man with a fearsome reputation, and survive, even earning the king's respect. Hereward has become the subject of romantic stories of Anglo-Saxon resistance to the Norman Conquest. In later centuries, he was positioned as the Last of the English, yet all of the evidence of Hereward's family and background suggests he was of Danish descent. He represented those who had settled in England generations earlier as part of that North Sea connection that was severed in 1066. It was not only Anglo-Saxon England that fought for survival but also Anglo-Danish England. The two worlds, though, were doomed in the face of the blossoming Norman world as a new England, closely connected to France, was forged in the place of the one previously connected to Scandinavia and northern Germany.

Chapter 2

Norman England

A history of castles : Castles arrive in England : William the
Conqueror's plans for the inheritance of his sons : Tensions between
the three sons of the Conqueror : The death of William Rufus :
Henry I becomes king : Henry conquers Normandy from his brother :
The White Ship Disaster : Henry I's succession plans

The Normans brought a Continental innovation that was almost unheard of in England: the castle. A few motte and bailey castles may have earned interested and suspicious looks before 1066. By 1051, Richard's Castle in Shropshire boasted a polygonal keep on a raised hill – the motte – surrounded by a defensible area, usually encircled by a wooden palisade – the bailey. This was built by a Norman, Richard Scrob, on land granted to him by Edward the Confessor. The small number of these constructions emerging before the Conquest illustrated Edward's own Norman connections.

The use of ditches and stone walls to defend a place was not new, though the creation of the motte, often a man-made, raised mound, was an innovation of medieval builders. Castles began to spread across continental Europe in the 9th and 10th centuries. Italy had an early explosion of construction that spread more slowly into modern Germany and France. These were primarily wooden buildings, though the Iberian Peninsula, modern Spain

and Portugal, saw early stone castles due to the relative scarcity of timber and the influence of Muslim architecture in the region.

As the Carolingian Empire, founded by Charlemagne at the turn of the 9th century, began to fracture at the end of that century, law and order in northern Europe broke down. Government became decentralised, and local lords took over responsibility for securing their regions. Castles became a centre for local government as well as the home of the magnate controlling the area. They were places that could be defended, and which could house a garrison to enforce law and order as well as military control. The spread of castles may suggest that warfare, particularly between local barons, was widespread. It also demonstrates the willingness of those nobles both to fill the vacuum left by the removal of central authority and to take advantage of an opportunity to increase their own power.

The Norman Conquest saw an explosion in castle construction in England. The previously scarce buildings began to dominate landscapes and communities. William, now King William I of England, the Conqueror, needed to impose the rule of a small minority onto the majority population. Castles, then relatively commonplace in his native Normandy and across France, offered the perfect solution. The scarcity of them in England meant that the Anglo-Saxons were poorly prepared to oppose authority wielded from behind castle walls. Warfare in Anglo-Saxon England had revolved around shield wall formations on the battlefield. Siege tactics were not something the English had been required to develop or learn.

'The fortifications that the Normans called castles were scarcely known in the English provinces, and so the English – in spite of their courage and love of fighting – could put up only a weak resistance to their enemies.' Norman chronicler Orderic Vitalis, c. (1140)

William set about constructing wooden fortifications as soon as he landed at Pevensey in 1066. Once he had won the Crown, he began parcelling out control of parts of England to his leading supporters. They built castles in their new domains both to protect themselves from a hostile local population and to enforce their new authority. The first iterations were usually wooden motte and bailey constructions. These were relatively quick and easy to build. On contested frontiers like the Welsh border, they were rebuilt in stone quickly in reaction to an almost constant threat. Ludlow Castle in Shropshire on the border with Wales was founded in 1075 and was being rebuilt in stone by the 1080s. Across England, stone structures replaced wood as the Norman Conquest became established. Like the castles, the new rulers were going nowhere. Over the next century and a half, around 1,000 castles sprang up across England and Wales.

The Castle in England

The castle became one of the primary methods of imposing Norman control on the English population. As well as in contested border areas, they were built in the centre of towns to dominate populations there too. Lincoln Castle was established in 1068 using the location of a Roman fort, incorporating some of the Roman walls into the fortifications. The Vikings had used Lincoln as a trading centre for the same reasons the Romans had built a fortress there. It was a meeting point for several significant roads and rivers. That made it an ideal location for a castle that could control several paths into and out of the north of England. The Domesday Book would record that 166 buildings, described as 'unoccupied residences', were torn down to make way for the new castle.

As they were reborn in stone, by the 12th century castles began

to take on many of the features familiar today. The donjon, more often known as the keep today, became commonplace. It was a large, usually rectangular building in the centre of the complex. The donjon began as the lord's home and a place to store treasure and later valuable prisoners. The donjon would eventually move underground, but remained a place to keep things locked up tight: the dungeon. The ditches at the bottom of the motte remained and became moats, sometimes filled with water but often still a dry defensive ditch. Stone walls began to replace the wooden palisades, with towers to guard them and ramparts to provide protection for defenders.

Over the centuries that followed, castles would evolve further into lavish, comfortable residences. They were often built with comfort in mind since they were to be the homes of the nobility, but, as their military use reduced, the focus on aesthetics and comfort grew. Castles remain a tangible link to the Norman Conquest of England. Their locations can give away the reason that they were built, and their endurance is a lingering testament to the determination of a foreign elite to subdue the population.

William the Conqueror ruled a dual realm separated by the Channel for 21 years. In 1085, he ordered the creation of the Domesday Book. It recorded who owned land throughout England, what its value was, and what they owed to the Crown for it. More than 13,000 places are named and over a quarter of a million households are noted, which suggests an estimated population of around one and a half million people. The Domesday Book, a name given to the project in the following century because its judgements could not be questioned, gave William vital information. Aside from understanding the size and wealth of his kingdom, it helped William understand how many men he could expect to raise if he needed an army. The Anglo-Saxon Chronicle recorded the annoyance this intrusion caused:

> 'So very narrowly, indeed, did he commission them to trace it out, that there was not one single hide, nor a yard of land, nay, moreover (it is shameful to tell, though he thought it no shame to do it), not even an ox, nor a cow, nor a swine was there left, that was not set down in his writ.'

This unprecedented project was completed in 1086, but a year later, King William I died. Accounts of his fate are unclear and differ from source to source. Some claim that, while fighting on the Norman borders, he either fell or crashed into the pommel of his saddle and died from the injury caused. The Norman monk Orderic Vitalis records another version of events, in which 'King William, who was very corpulent, fell sick from the excessive heat and his great fatigues'. He died six weeks later, on 9 September 1087. Whatever the true

LISTEN TO THE
PODCAST

The Story of
Castles

cause of his death, Orderic noted that 'His death was worthy of his life'. That was meant as a compliment, but at William's funeral in Caen his body proved too large for the hole provided. As the mourners tried to cram the corpse in, it burst, releasing fluids and a terrible stench into the abbey.

The First Norman Succession

William left his duchy of Normandy to his oldest son Robert. Since the duchy's foundation by Vikings, dukes of Normandy had been vassals of the King of Franks (a title that would later become King of France). His next surviving son became King William II (otherwise known as William Rufus) of England. The youngest son, Henry, received £5,000 in cash. The reasons for the division of his property in this way are debated. William I and Robert had a difficult relationship. Robert is known as Curthose, meaning 'short stockings', which was reportedly a derogatory nickname given to him by his father. Robert did not get on well with his brothers either. In one childhood incident, William and Henry played a prank on their older brother that involved tipping a full chamber pot on his head. When Robert told their father, he received no sympathy.

This Norman system is the practice William the Conqueror followed. It doesn't mean that he excluded Robert from the Crown of England because he disliked him. In this case, what William had won in his lifetime was deemed more valuable than his patrimony, so the settlement looks imbalanced. Still, that doesn't preclude a bad relationship between father and son. Orderic Vitalis's account places a long speech into William's mouth on his deathbed. On the subject of Robert, he supposedly said, 'I know for certain that the country which is subject to his dominion will be truly wretched. He is a proud and silly prodigal, and will have long to suffer severe misfortune.' Ouch.

Dividing the Kingdom of England from the Duchy of Normandy created problems. Since the Conquest, those who owned lands on both sides of the Channel would be forced to serve two masters rather than one, splitting their loyalties. The desire for a single ruler would dominate succession disputes for decades to follow and was an important consideration for any candidate hoping to gain control. Robert and William II made an agreement on their father's death that, unless they had sons, each would recognise the other as his heir. The arrangement fell apart less than a year after their father's death.

Concerned about their conflicting loyalties to rival brothers, the barons preferred to reunite England and Normandy. Bishop Odo of Bayeux, the half-brother of William the Conqueror, led the rebels, who decided to oust William from England in favour

PRIMOGENITURE

Primogeniture is the right of succession by a firstborn child. In a medieval context, that meant the oldest son. A daughter could inherit land if they had no brothers, but it would usually then be managed by her husband.

Patrimony refers to the lands, estates and titles inherited from a father or another male ancestor.

Inheritance was dealt with in different ways by different cultures. Normandy preferred the French tradition that the oldest son received the patrimony. A second son would receive anything added to the patrimony during the father's lifetime by marriage, purchase or conquest. Younger sons might be destined for a career in the Church. This system avoided the dividing and dwindling of a family's power.

of Robert. Their selection may have been the result of Robert's reputation as a bit of a softy whom they could manipulate more easily. The rebellion began at Easter in 1088 in England. Robert's forces strengthened their castles and began attacking the king's allies. William responded by offering cash and land to anyone who abandoned Robert while promising to improve his government. He also attacked some of the rebels, capturing his uncle Bishop Odo at Pevensey Castle. William's multi-pronged assault worked. The revolt collapsed. It had not been helped by Robert's failure to arrive in England as bad weather kept his ships in port in Normandy. William was, Orderic Vitalis recalls, counselled to forgive the rebels since 'He who is your enemy now, may be your useful friend another time.'

Sibling Rivalry

As part of the effort to raise rebellion in 1088, Robert had asked his little brother Henry to lend him some of the cash he had inherited. Henry refused, but they reached an agreement by which Robert sold Henry lands across the Cotentin Peninsula that extended over much of western Normandy.

The title Count of the Cotentin was created for Henry at a cost of £3,000. It was a good way for a landless third son to invest his money. When Robert faced a revolt in Normandy centred on Rouen, its capital, in 1090, Henry came to his aid, leading forces to defeat the rebels. Having captured the leader, Conan Pilatus, Henry had him taken to the top of a tower in Rouen Castle. Despite Conan's pleading and offers of a vast ransom, he was thrown from the tower to his death as an example to others who might oppose their duke.

Robert responded by ejecting Henry from the city, perhaps because his little brother's success made Robert look bad. When

William invaded Normandy in 1091, Robert was forced to negotiate. He gave his brother some lands in Normandy in return for
a promise to help him settle the duchy. They sealed the Treaty
of Rouen, which again recognised each as the heir to the other's
lands and titles while they had no sons. The arrangement included
the brothers ganging up on Henry to take back the lands Robert
had sold him. Henry was besieged within Mont St Michel in the
spring and was forced to surrender, after which he was forced out
of Normandy altogether.

In 1092, Henry returned to Normandy and captured
Domfront. Over the next two years, he rebuilt his network of
support across western Normandy. In 1095, the First Crusade
was called by Pope Urban II. Robert signed up immediately and
mortgaged Normandy to William to fund the expedition. He
would have great success in the Holy Land, turning around his
floundering reputation in Europe. When he came home in 1100,
he got something of a shock.

On 2 August 1100, William II was doing what Norman kings
always enjoyed most. He was hunting with his friends in the
New Forest. The hunt was a favourite sporting pastime that not
only allowed the practice of riding and fighting techniques but
also reinforced the social hierarchy. In 1070, a brother between
Robert and William in age, Richard, had been killed in a hunting
accident in the New Forest when he hit a low branch. Lightning
was about to strike the family for a second time.

During the hunt in 1100, William was struck by a stray arrow
fired by one of his companions. The arrow punctured the king's
lung, and it was clear to those with him that he was beyond help.
They unceremoniously left the king's body on the forest floor and
fled back to their lands to prepare for whatever trouble was to
come. William had no sons, so there would be a succession crisis.
It was left to a local arrow maker to find the king's corpse and
take it to Winchester for burial, where his remains are believed

to be in one of the mortuary chests displayed within Winchester Cathedral.

Among the king's hunting party was his little brother Henry, with whom he had grown to be on good terms. Henry rushed from his dying brother, heading straight for Winchester, then the site of the royal treasury and still an important political city. It had once been the capital of the Anglo-Saxon Kingdom of Wessex, and retained some of its former importance. At Winchester, Henry claimed the English throne. Some, led by William de Breteuil, opposed him, citing oaths they and Henry had sworn to accept the arrangement that made Robert the rightful king. Henry argued that he was the only son of the Conqueror born 'in the purple', meaning to a reigning king. The term referred to the Byzantine principle of porphyrogeniture, literally meaning 'born in the purple', which favoured those born while their father was Emperor. The chamber set aside for Empresses in labour was decorated in imperial purple. Hence those born in the room were born in the purple.

Henry employed this argument in England in 1100 because it favoured his cause. He managed to impose his will on those who resisted, and the keys to the treasury were handed over. On 5 August, just three days after his brother's death, Henry was crowned in Westminster Abbey. He issued a Coronation Charter, also known as a Charter of Liberties. It promised to enforce law and order and respect the independence of the Church. Significantly, it made several references to the laws of Edward the Confessor, so seemed to offer a return to something closer to Anglo-Saxon rule. As a result of being born after the Conquest, Henry was also the only one of his brothers born in England. One of his first acts upon becoming king was to marry Matilda of Scotland. She was a great-granddaughter of Edmund Ironside, making her a descendant of the House of Wessex as well as the Kings of Scotland. Henry was doing all that he could to appear English, promising a reversal of the Norman Conquest.

When Robert returned to Normandy from the First Crusade, he found William had died and Henry had been crowned King of England. Furious, he set about preparing to invade England. He was assisted by the arrival of Ranulf Flambard, who had served William the Conqueror and William Rufus, but had been imprisoned by Henry. Ranulf holds the dubious honour of being the first named prisoner held at the Tower of London. He was also the first prisoner to escape from the Tower. Accounts tell how he got his guards drunk at a feast and then used a rope that had been smuggled in at the bottom of one of the barrels of wine to climb down from a window.

In July 1101, Robert landed at Portsmouth with an invasion force. He came face to face with his brother at Alton in Hampshire, but, rather than fight, they negotiated the Treaty of Alton. The terms required Robert to recognise Henry as king and drop his claim to the Crown. In return, Henry would pay his brother £2,000 a year and give up his own claim to Normandy.

The treaty also renewed the arrangement between William and Robert that, if either man died without an heir, their brother would inherit from them. It sounded good but would not last for long.

Despite the agreement, Henry fomented unrest in Normandy from 1103. When it was sufficiently destabilised in 1106, he arrived with an army, offering to restore the peace his brother had allowed to crumble. On 28 September 1106, the two brothers faced each other on the battlefield. Robert began the engagement with a cavalry charge, doubtless feeling confident after his military experiences in the Holy Land. Fighting raged for around an hour before Robert's force broke and began to flee. The duke was taken prisoner by his little brother and forced to order the surrender of Normandy to Henry.

The willingness of the Norman barony to support Henry reflected their desire to retain a single lord across their territories. Henry had the advantage of being a crowned and anointed king, a position that could not be unmade while he was alive. Robert was a duke and one who, thanks to Henry's meddling, had demonstrated his inability to control Normandy. Henry's offer to reunite his father's lands and end the tricky division of loyalty suited the nobility. The king had played on their concerns and desires perfectly. Robert was imprisoned at Devizes Castle in Wiltshire for 20 years before being moved to Cardiff Castle. During his enforced retirement he learned Welsh and developed a reputation for writing poetry, but would never be freed. Robert died in February 1134, aged around 83. He is buried in Gloucester Cathedral, where a wooden effigy of him created a century after his death can still be seen today.

Uniting the Norman Inheritance

Henry now held England and Normandy as one realm. The one lingering problem for him was that by the time of his capture Robert had a son. William Clito was three years old in 1106 and was placed into the custody of one of Henry's allies. The name Clito was a Norman version of the Anglo-Saxon term ætheling, meaning throneworthy. He would prove a thorn in his uncle's side in years to come. Henry consolidated his position and developed a reputation as a hard ruler, a trait largely admired in the medieval period. Kings were expected to be fair, but ruthless in maintaining law and order on behalf of their subjects. In 1119, Henry oversaw an exchange of hostages between his son-in-law, Eustace, and a rival. When Eustace proceeded to blind the hostage he had been given, Henry permitted two of his daughters to be blinded and have their noses cut off. The two girls were the king's own granddaughters. In 1124, when soldiers complained that they had been paid in substandard silver coins, Henry ordered the Bishop of Salisbury to investigate. Those found guilty of debasing the coinage had their hands and genitals cut off. This kind of measure was widely approved of by Henry's contemporaries.

A dubious record that Henry I still holds is that he had more known illegitimate children than any other monarch. By various mistresses, the king had at least 22 illegitimate children and possibly several more. Despite this, Henry fathered only two legitimate children with his queen Matilda of Scotland. Henry's father had been illegitimate, which posed no obstacle to taking the dukedom of Normandy or conquering a kingdom. However, once on the throne only legitimate children, specifically sons, were considered capable of succession. Henry's oldest child was a daughter, Matilda. Born in 1102, she was sent to marry the Holy Roman Emperor Henry V in 1114, taking the title Empress Matilda, which she would retain for the rest of her life. Henry's only legitimate son was William Adelin, born in 1103. Adelin is another variation of the notion of a title meaning throneworthy.

The White Ship Disaster

Tragedy struck for King Henry I during the night of 25 November 1120. With his court and many family members, Henry had been in Normandy. He was due to return to England to prepare to celebrate Christmas there. When his preparations were fairly advanced, a man named Thomas FitzStephen begged an audience with the king. Henry saw the man, who explained that his father had been the master of the ship that had carried the king's father across the Channel on his way to conquering England. Thomas had a newly fitted-out ship named *La Blanche-Nef*, the White Ship. It was, Thomas said, beautiful and swift. He asked for the honour of taking the king across to England, sharing the experience of both of their fathers. Henry declined because he did not wish to change his plans so late, but suggested that Thomas might take William and his young friends instead.

Bursting with pride, Thomas prepared his ship. As the young men and women piled on board, the prince ordered huge quantities of wine to be brought for them and the crew. Several men, including the prince's cousin Stephen of Blois, disembarked as things got rowdy. Contemporary estimates suggest there were around 300 people on board as the White Ship moved out of Barfleur harbour in the darkness of the late evening. Priests who brought holy water to bless the voyage were shoved away as soldiers took to the oars to try to speed the boat up, thinking they could overtake the king's ship, which had left earlier. The drunken crew, passengers and navigator hadn't cleared the harbour when the side of the new ship ground against a rock that was a well-known danger point. Sober sailors would never have struck it. With its side ripped away, the White Ship sank beneath the waves with terrifying speed. Some accounts say the prince made it into a lifeboat but, on hearing one of his half-sisters crying for help, ordered it turned round, only to be swamped by those trying to climb aboard.

Two men remained above water. A butcher named Berold was saved by his cheap but warm fleece coat. A young nobleman named Geoffrey also clung to a floating piece of the ship. At some point in the cold night, Thomas bobbed to the surface. He asked the two men where the prince was. On hearing that he had drowned, the captain allowed himself to slip beneath the icy waters, preferring death to explaining what had happened to the king. By morning, Geoffrey had also been lost to the black seas and only Berold the butcher, who had been on board to chase debts he was owed by the court, had survived. His poor clothing had saved him when the rich, thin silks of the young nobles had done them no good. In England, some had thought they had heard screams drifting on the night air from the sea. When word finally arrived of the disaster, none dared inform the king. Nobles stifled their own tears so the king would not ask why they were distraught.

LISTEN TO THE
PODCAST

The White Ship

Eventually, a young boy was pushed before the king to tell him that several of his children, including his only legit-imate son, were dead. Henry collapsed to his knees and had to be carried from the room. Orderic Vitalis talked of the king's grief in biblical terms. 'Not Jacob was

more woe-stricken for the loss of Joseph, nor did David give vent to more woeful lamentations for the murder of Ammon or Absalom.' Personal grief was made heavier by the dynastic problems that threatened to engulf Henry's reign. His queen had died two years earlier, and he would remarry but would not have any children with his second wife.

William Clito was now considered by many as the natural heir to his father, Robert, and uncle, Henry. When the Count of

Flanders died without an heir in 1127, Louis VI of France gave the wealthy county, just to the east of Normandy, to William to provide a platform for his claim to be Henry's heir. It was close to the English coast and a key trading partner of the kingdom, so it strengthened William's position. Henry had no intention of allowing the Crown to slip from his line. None among his brood of illegitimate children were an option, though particularly the oldest, Robert, Earl of Gloucester, would have been a strong candidate if his parentage had been right. Five years after the White Ship Disaster, with no sign of a son arriving from his second marriage, Empress Matilda's husband died. In 1125, Matilda was 23 and had not been in England or Normandy for 11 years. Henry called her home and began to rebuild his shattered plans around her.

Female rule was an issue in France and England during this period. Henry had no real option but to impose it on England and Normandy. In January 1127, he caused all of his barons present at his Christmas court to swear to recognise Matilda as his successor on his death. According to the chronicler William of Malmesbury, each of them gave their oath that 'they would immediately and without hesitation accept his daughter Matilda, formerly empress, as their lady'. As William Clito became more active on the Continent, Henry married his daughter to Geoffrey Plantagenet, Count of Anjou, who controlled lands on Normandy's southern border. The Angevins were frequent enemies of the Normans, but it was a powerful diplomatic alliance against William. Matilda was 25, and Geoffrey was just 14. She was outraged by the match, not least because he was a mere count while she was an empress. She insulted her new husband by insisting on retaining the title her first spouse had given her and left Anjou to return to her father in protest.

Within weeks of this new political alliance, William Clito died, in July 1128. The couple managed to resolve their differences and went on to have a son named Henry (the Young Henry) in 1133. King Henry I appears then to have hoped he might live long enough for his grandson to succeed him and avoid the problem of female rule, particularly as Matilda and Geoffrey's new-found unity came at the cost of their relationship with her father. On 1 December 1135, at the age of about 67, Henry I died at a hunting lodge at Lyon-la-

LISTEN TO THE
PODCAST

Empress Matilda

Forêt. A chronicler, Henry of Huntingdon, recorded that he died from a surfeit of lampreys – he ate too much of his favourite dish, a delicacy in Henry's time, similar to eels.

Chapter 3

The Anarchy and the Rise of the Plantagenets

The accession of King Stephen : Empress Matilda presses
her claim : How medieval warfare was conducted : King Stephen
is captured : Matilda's husband conquers Normandy : The Empress
prepares for her coronation as Lady of the English : The release
of Stephen : Henry FitzEmpress takes up his mother's cause :
The end of the Anarchy : The Angevin Empire : The Becket Affair :
Henry II's sons rebel : The death of Henry II

Henry I had made his plans for what would happen after his death. He had extracted oaths from his barons to recognise and support his daughter, Empress Matilda. Given that he had ignored a similar arrangement between his own brothers, Henry might reasonably have been concerned about what would actually happen. Indeed Empress Matilda did not become England's new ruler. Instead, her cousin Stephen of Blois, Count of Boulogne, raced across the Channel and was crowned at Westminster Abbey on 22 December 1135. The three weeks it took him to gain control of the royal treasury at Winchester (helped by the fact that his brother was Bishop of Winchester) and to be accepted as king might seem slow in comparison to Henry I's three days, yet it proved a controversial and important step, for a number of reasons.

The interregnum, although relatively brief, was still a moment in which law and order broke down. Norman chroniclers complained the people 'abandon themselves to robbery and pillage; they butcher one another', while in England another writer lamented that there was 'treason in these lands; for every man that might robbed another'. The situation was further aggravated by David I, King of Scots crossing the border and taking Wark, Alnwick, Norham and Newcastle in the wake of Henry's death. Furthermore, Empress Matilda and her husband Geoffrey were militarily active on the Norman border. They had been in dispute with Henry about some castles they claimed ownership of when he died. This fed into stories that the old king had disinherited his daughter on his deathbed and made his favourite nephew Stephen his heir. Whatever the case, Empress Matilda did not rush to England. In fact, she perhaps could not, as she was pregnant with her third son at the time. Stephen was able to be in the right place at the right time.

Those within London also saw an opportunity in 1135 to regain some of the power lost at the Norman Conquest in 1066. The anonymous writer of the *Gesta Stephani* – the Deeds of Stephen – recorded that 'the elders and those most shrewd in counsel summoned an assembly, and taking prudent forethought for the state of the kingdom, on their own initiative, they agreed unanimously to choose a king'. This effort to reassert the powers that had been held by the Witan to elect a monarch meant Stephen was chosen and underwent a coronation. In Normandy, there was no desire to recognise Henry's daughter either. A council of barons at Neubourg was on the brink of offering the duchy to Stephen's older brother, Theobald, Count of Blois, when envoys arrived with news of the coronation in England. The preference for a single lord across the regions surfaced again. In embarrassing scenes, Theobald was told he had lost the post to his little brother.

Empress Matilda had no intention of taking the theft of her inheritance lightly. The 19-year period of King Stephen's reign is remembered as the Anarchy. The Anglo-Saxon Chronicle famously bemoaned the civil war and lawlessness during the period. 'Wheresoever men tilled, the earth bore no corn, for the land was all ruined by such deeds; and they said openly that Christ and his saints were asleep. Such and more than we can say we endured nineteen winters for our sins.' Empress Matilda would press her claim to England, and her husband Geoffrey did all he could to conquer Normandy. King David was initially driven back but soon took more land in northern England that he controlled for the rest of Stephen's reign. The word 'anarchy' is misleading, though. England would be ruled by three separate power blocks but would not be ungoverned or anarchic.

The Empress Invades

After an early failure in Normandy, Matilda placed her claim before the Pope for his adjudication in April 1139. Stephen's rebuttal was a scandalous claim that Matilda was illegitimate because her mother had been a nun. This was an old story, resurrected to discredit the Empress. Pope Innocent II dodged making a decision and simply refused to hear the case. He wrote to confirm the legitimacy of Stephen's kingship since a coronation was sacred and could not be undone, but he did not deny Matilda's claim. On 30 September 1139, Empress Matilda landed in England to press her cause in person. She arrived at Arundel Castle on the south coast, which belonged to the Earl of Sussex, the new husband of Matilda's stepmother. When the king arrived at the castle, he agreed to allow Matilda safe conduct to her half-brother Robert, Earl of Gloucester, at his castle in Bristol.

The previous year, Robert had entered open rebellion against Stephen. He had issued a diffidatio, a 'defiance', which meant

SIEGE CODES OF CONDUCT

Sieges had their own code of conduct. The defenders would be offered the opportunity to surrender without loss of life. They were entitled to appeal to their overlord for help, and a deadline would be set for that assistance to arrive. If it did, the attackers might withdraw or give battle. If it failed to materialise, the defenders were given a further chance to surrender the castle. If they agreed, they would be allowed to leave unharmed. If they refused, and chose to try to see off the siege, then they could expect no mercy. All within the castle could be executed if it fell.

that he had renounced his allegiance to the king and recognised no lord. Robert claimed he did this in response to an attempt on his life organised by Stephen in Normandy. Now holed up at the impenetrable Bristol Castle, Robert was a nuisance rather than a threat. Stephen was criticised by contemporaries for allowing Matilda to travel to Robert, but his options were limited. Attacking a woman was hardly chivalrous, and Stephen is reported as expressing his preference to have all his enemies in one place rather than spread around his kingdom. Whatever the rationale, the outcome was years of entrenched and bitter struggles along the fringes of areas controlled by Stephen and those now backing Matilda.

Medieval warfare centred around laying siege to castles. The standard military handbook of the day was *De Re Militari* – On Military Matters. It was a treatise written in the late 4th century by Vegetius that was designed to present all of the things the Roman Empire had done well militarily and the lessons to be learned from its failures. One of the core tenets of *De Re Militari* is that pitched battles should be avoided whenever possible. Although he provides instructions for how to engage the enemy, Vegetius warns it is 'a conjecture full of uncertainty and fatal to kingdoms and nations'. This wisdom held sway for a millennium, resulting in siege warfare as castles became widespread.

This method of often slow, ponderous warfare prevailed during most of the medieval period. Much of the notion of anarchy may be the result of the chronicle accounts available for the period. Many were based in the southwest of England, on the front line of this conflict. It may have felt to them like this was what was happening the length and breadth of the country. The Anglo-Saxon Chronicle's lament was

LISTEN TO THE
PODCAST

Deception and Trickery in Medieval Warfare

written in Peterborough, where Hugh Bigod, Earl of Norfolk, frequently sparked trouble for his own gain. Another chronicle was written at Lincoln, the location of the period's only pitched battle. The skewed view of chroniclers has contributed to a view of Stephen's reign as relentlessly chaotic, which it was not. Monastic growth in England during Stephen's reign was explosive, and the monks writing about being unable to walk down the road safely were able to set up new monasteries and travel across the country to fill them.

The moment of real crisis and action came in 1141. Stephen was at Lincoln to try to resolve a dispute with the Earl of Chester, who had snatched Lincoln Castle. The earl was the son-in-law of Robert, Earl of Gloucester and appealed to him for help. On 2 February 1141, Robert arrived with an army. Stephen was advised by some of his men to retreat, but he refused. He may have been affected by the reputation of his father, who was branded a coward for fleeing the siege of Antioch in 1097. He resolved to fight.

DIVISIONS OF THE ROYAL ARMY

The royal army was divided into the traditional three sections, or battles. The vanguard was the first portion to engage or would take the right flank if arranged in a single line. The main battle was in the middle and would reinforce the vanguard or join the fighting at the appropriate time. The rearguard remained at the back as further reinforcements and to protect from attack from behind, or took the left wing if forming a single line.

The First Battle of Lincoln

As the fighting began, Robert's vanguard gained the initiative and parts of Stephen's army began to retreat. The king himself refused to leave and was eventually left with a few comrades, surrounded by Robert's men. Chroniclers describe Stephen fighting 'like a lion, grinding his teeth and foaming at the mouth like a boar'. He broke his weapon and had to grab another until eventually he was overwhelmed and taken captive. Stephen was taken to the Empress, at Gloucester, where he was placed in chains and locked in a cell as Matilda set about taking control of the kingdom. Matilda settled on taking the title Lady of the English. It avoided using 'queen', which had come to mean the wife of a king rather than a woman who ruled. Lady of the English harked back to the Anglo-Saxon daughter of Alfred the Great, Æthelflæd, who had ruled the Kingdom of Mercia as Lady of the Mercians.

In Normandy, Stephen's fall saw Matilda's husband Geoffrey enter the duchy and begin to take control. In England, progress was slow. Only in March did Matilda enter Winchester, after negotiations with the bishop, Stephen's brother. She then had to wait until 24 June to gain permission to access London. At this point, the chroniclers turned on Matilda with unveiled misogyny. Matilda asked for loans from London merchants, who refused. She complained that they had always lent Stephen money and insisted they do the same for her. Amidst her efforts to establish herself, chroniclers unanimously turned on her. They grumbled that she failed to stand when her brother Robert, her uncle David, King of Scots, or Henry, Bishop of Winchester entered the room, none of whom would have been considered senior to a king of England. They complained that she would not be led by men, that she 'arranged everything as she herself thought fit and according to her own arbitrary will'. When she spoke, it was 'not with unassuming gentleness, but with a voice of authority', with 'every trace of a woman's gentleness removed from her face'.

It is hard to imagine a man awaiting his coronation facing the same criticism. Matilda's father Henry I had been a hard man, which had been lauded as how a king ought to behave. Before and after this moment in 1141, chroniclers viewed Empress Matilda as an impressive figure, and this lies at the heart of the issue she faced. A medieval ruler was required primarily to provide security for his people. That meant leading armies into the field or undertaking sieges, but women were not permitted to perform that role. It was a problem medieval noblemen were unable (or unwilling) to get their minds around. If someone, her husband Geoffrey or half-brother Robert, led Matilda's armies, would they not be the real king? The complexity of this question contributed to the shunning of female rule in medieval England for a further four centuries.

As Empress Matilda prepared for her imminent coronation, an army arrived in London led by another woman named Matilda. This was Queen Matilda, Stephen's wife. She had seen

the way the Empress had been treated, and sprang a perfectly constructed trap. The queen had already visited London to ask for her husband's release, though not the return of his Crown, and for recognition of their son Eustace's inheritance from her. Empress Matilda had refused. This had been calculated to cause concern about the Empress's attitude to inheritance. Her dispute with Stephen had nothing to do with the lawful inheritance of a maternal title, in this case as Count of Boulogne. In denying the request, the Empress made nobles and barons nervous. On the eve of the coronation, Queen Matilda arrived with an army to demonstrate that a woman could do it if it were on behalf of a man – her husband or son.

Chroniclers describe the queen's force flooding through the streets of London like bees. They burst into the place where the Empress was dining but found she had left, alerted to the danger. The men were able to sit down and enjoy a hot feast, though, so close had they come to their quarry. Empress Matilda retreated to Winchester and the royal army pursued her. When the Bishop of Winchester also turned on the Empress, she was forced to withdraw from there too. As her half-brother Robert covered her retreat, he was captured. Frantic negotiations followed. Robert tried to insist that his release was not worth that of a king, but Empress Matilda knew she was in trouble without her military commander. Eventually, it was agreed that Stephen would be exchanged for Robert. On 1 November 1135, King Stephen was released. His capture had been seen as God's judgement on him, and his release represented the return of divine favour and a bolstering of the institution of the Crown, which had proven itself able to survive captivity for most of a year.

In 1141, Empress Matilda had been on the brink of becoming the first queen regnant of England. By the end of the year, Stephen's position was enhanced, and it was clear she would never rule. Siege warfare that saw little territory gained or lost by either side recommenced. Empress Matilda seemed to now have to turn her attention to keeping a claim alive on behalf of her oldest son, Henry. Robert, Earl of Gloucester died on 31 October 1147. Deprived of her closest supporter and military leader, Empress Matilda left England in early 1148.

Meanwhile, on the Continent, her husband Geoffrey had been making slow but solid progress into Normandy. In 1144, he had taken the capital city of Rouen and been proclaimed Duke of Normandy. Once again, the kingdom and duchy were fractured from each other, and those noblemen with lands on either side of the Channel were put in a difficult situation. In 1150, at the age of 17, Henry FitzEmpress, as he was frequently called (Fitz denoting 'son of'), was handed Normandy by his father. It was part of the kindling to reignite the claim to England that his mother Matilda had kept smouldering for him. King Stephen would now have to face down another threat to his Crown from the grandson of Henry I.

The Next Generation

Henry FitzEmpress was born on 5 March 1133 at Le Mans. He had first set foot in England in November 1142 aged nine. His uncle Robert, Earl of Gloucester had visited Normandy to ask for Geoffrey's help in England. Geoffrey's only offer was to allow Robert to take his heir across the Channel. The one benefit this provided to Empress Matilda's cause was to remind those loyal to her that she had a son who might one day take up her father's legacy. Almost as soon as they landed in England, Robert was able to take castles at Wareham, Lulworth and on the Isle of Portland. It was a hands-on demonstration of the power of taking castles quickly for young Henry. Henry spent just over a year in England, his military education supplemented by an academic

one led by the well-respected Adelard of Bath. Both were taken seriously. One courtier would later write that Henry was 'ignorant of nothing which befitteth a gentleman, well-learned for all the demands of social intercourse and practical affairs, having knowledge of all the languages which are spoken from the Bay of Biscay to the Jordan'.

When Geoffrey took Normandy, Henry was summoned home. He would next cross to England in 1147. At the age of 15, Henry gathered a vast army, filled ships with treasure to pay more soldiers, and landed on the south coast. At least, that was what the rumour mill reported. After a few days it became clear the teenager merely had a handful of knights, a few mercenaries promised their pay in plunder, and had not consulted his parents about invading England. They failed to make an impression at Cricklade Castle or Purton Castle before Henry gave in. With no plunder, honour demanded that he pay his men. When Empress Matilda refused to help her son because he had not sought her approval for the action, he tried his uncle Robert, who also refused. In an astonishing display of bravado, Henry then asked King Stephen, whose kingdom he had invaded, to bail him out. To the shock of many contemporaries, Stephen agreed and paid Henry's small band. This had the immediate advantage of causing the nuisance to leave but was something of a victory over Henry I's heir, and it may have created a well of sympathy and respect between the two that would affect their future interaction.

In January 1153, now 19 years old, Henry came to England for the third time. He was now Duke of Normandy, the title handed over by his father in 1151. Geoffrey had died unexpectedly on 7 September that year at the age of 38, making Henry Count of Anjou, Maine and Touraine. His father's death had come as Henry was preparing an invasion, despite any sympathy Stephen's generosity may have fostered, which had to be abandoned. In spring 1152, as he prepared another assault, Henry received an offer of marriage from Eleanor of Aquitaine. He sped south, and the two were married on 18 May, less than two months after Eleanor's marriage to King Louis VII of France had been annulled. Eleanor was probably 28 (her year of birth was most likely 1104, but may have been 1102). Aged 19, Henry was now in control of western France from the Channel to the Pyrenees mountains. He swiftly returned to his invasion plans, adding Duke of Aquitaine to his list of titles, but was dragged away once more by trouble on the Norman border.

The long-anticipated invasion came in January 1153. Henry attacked Wallingford, joined by his English allies, and King Stephen arrived with an army in response. They camped on either

side of the River Avon, but in the morning the king withdrew, blaming the swollen waters of the river. A great deal of careful manoeuvring followed that saw Henry take towns and castles in the Midlands, but a head-to-head encounter was avoided. Eventually, the stalemate caused the barons to encourage their masters to talk. An agreement was reached by which Stephen would remain king but would adopt Henry as his son and appoint him heir to the throne. Stephen's oldest son Eustace was, unsurprisingly, enraged by the talks. He vented his spleen by pillaging in the east of England, and promptly died. The settlement was published at Christmas 1153. Henry returned to his vast territories on the Continent.

King Stephen died on 25 October 1154 aged around 60. Henry did not rush to his coronation, perhaps allowing space for any enemies to show themselves. On Sunday 19 December 1154, Henry and Eleanor were crowned at Westminster Abbey. Henry quickly took advantage of a minority crisis in Scotland to take back the land King David had held for most of Stephen's reign. From the Pyrenees in the south, his domain now touched Hadrian's Wall in the north. Henry's main problem lay with his wife's first husband, King Louis VII, who increasingly viewed the young man as a danger to his own Crown. Louis had ended his marriage to Eleanor because she had 'failed' to provide him with a son, so embarrassment was added to fear when Eleanor gave birth to Henry's first son in August 1153 while Henry was campaigning in England. Although this child would sadly not survive, the couple went on to have four sons and three daughters. The boys would prove the bane of their father's life.

Henry II spent much of his reign tearing around his vast territories, keeping the peace. In England and Normandy, his primary concern and measure of his own success was Henry I. The new king committed to recovering all of the lands and rights enjoyed by his grandfather. Part of this effort included reversing changes

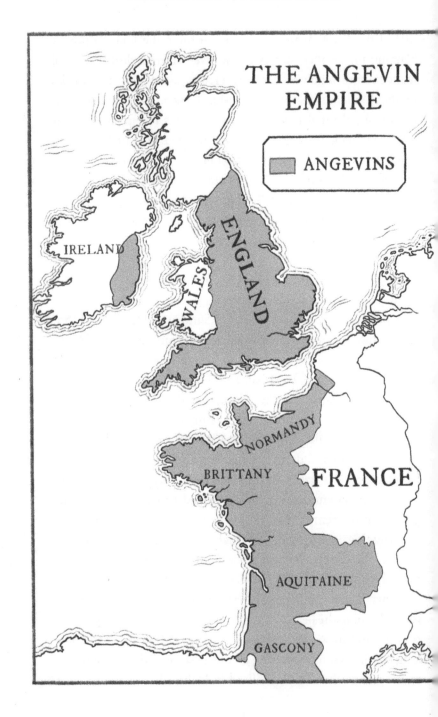

in the authority of the Church in England. Henry quickly formed a strong relationship with Thomas Becket, a gifted clerk who had become his Chancellor. The Chancellor headed up the king's writing office, preparing and sending correspondence. It was the most senior office in government, and Thomas was good at his job. Henry hated the showiness of kingship. In 1158, Henry and Eleanor spent Easter at Worcester and took part in a crown-wearing ceremony. Under Norman kings, these had become traditional at festivals such as Easter and Christmas. At the end of the ceremony, Henry removed his crown, placed it on the altar at Worcester Cathedral, and swore never to put one on again. There is no record of him ever breaking that vow.

The Thomas Becket Affair: Showman to Martyr

Thomas provided the sparkle that Henry had no interest in. For example, the Chancellor would hold lavish feasts, and Henry would return from a day of hunting, ride his horse into the Great Hall, leap into a chair and put his dusty boots up on the table. In the summer of 1158, Henry was negotiating a marriage between his heir, another Henry, and a daughter of Louis VII, who still lacked a son. He was not interested in making a grand entrance into Paris, so he sent Thomas. Parisians gawped as the Chancellor's procession arrived. It was led by 250 footmen, singing as they walked. A collection of hounds on leashes came next, ahead of eight large wagons that clattered along the road. Each was pulled by five carthorses, each horse ridden by a monkey, and each wagon guarded by chained mastiffs who jogged alongside. Two wagons were packed with barrels of beer. Behind the wagons, 28 pack-horses hauled gold and silver plate, cloth, books, relics and cash. Next came squires holding the reins of destriers, the war horses of knights. Astride each mount sat a knight in gleaming armour. Then there was an array of impressive birds of prey, the sons of barons placed into Thomas's household, and then his clerks and servants. Unaware of Henry's motivation, Paris was buzzing with expectation. If this was the King of England's Chancellor, imagine how splendid the king himself must be!

Henry hit upon an idea when the Archbishop of Canterbury died in 1161. If he put his friend and loyal servant Thomas in charge of the Church, he would be able to hand over the control of it that Henry coveted. Thomas objected to the scheme. He was just over 40, unmarried, had no children yet, and was enjoying the highest office in the land with all of its trappings. Becoming Archbishop of Canterbury brought prestige, but then he would be required to hand that away for ever. He would be prevented from having a family, and his legacy would be the subjugation of the Church in England. The king ignored Thomas's protests. Once installed as Archbishop of Canterbury, Thomas was summoned to approve the Constitutions of Clarendon in early 1164. To Henry's shock and fury, Thomas refused to accept what Henry presented as the traditional rights of the Crown in relation to the Church.

By October, Henry had arranged criminal charges against Thomas relating to his time as Chancellor, and summoned the archbishop to Northampton for his trial. Thomas coolly reminded the king that, on making him archbishop, Henry had given Thomas a pardon for anything he had ever done in Henry's service. The king was unimpressed. Thomas's defiance drew acclaim from some fellow churchmen, but others berated him for opposing the king's will. Warned that he was likely to be executed or murdered, Thomas fled, eventually reaching the court of King Louis VII.

The French king had been seeking ways to destabilise Henry. Not only had he personally embarrassed Louis by marrying his former wife, but Henry and Eleanor failed to seek Louis's permission for their union when they were both his vassals. Added to that, Eleanor had provided Henry with the sons Louis had blamed her for failing to give him. Beyond the personal, the rivalry was deeply political. Kings of France controlled a small area around Paris and relied on ties of fealty to extend their influence further across France. In England, the king owned all and, in legal terms, loaned it to prominent supporters. French kings coveted the same level of power but were yet to realise it. Henry owned more of France than Louis and all his other allies put together. For as long as he lacked a son at least, Louis must have feared whether Henry would come for the Crown of France as he had the English one.

Becket's arrival offered Louis the perfect opportunity to cause trouble. At that moment, the Pope was exiled from Rome and in Sens, within Louis's sphere of influence. Henry asked his fellow king not to allow Becket into his lands and to ask the Pope to ignore the archbishop. Louis had no intention of passing up such a prize. He sent word to Pope Alexander III, suggesting he offer Thomas a warm welcome. The Pope duly obliged. When Becket handed over a copy of the Constitutions of Clarendon, the Pope and his cardinals agreed the archbishop had done the right thing. Alexander excommunicated anyone who abided by Henry's document. In England, the king retaliated by making it treason to bring an edict from the Pope into his kingdom and banning clergy from leaving England without royal permission. It was tantamount to a break with the Roman Church.

Becket would be a thorn in Henry's side for the next six years. He was rarely the real focus of the king's attention; more of a nuisance who arrived at peace talks to throw the cat among the pigeons and disrupt Henry's plans. The king was infuriated when this did happen. In 1168, he wrote to Pope Alexander that he 'would sooner accept the errors of Nur al-Din and become an infidel, than suffer Thomas to hold sway in Canterbury Cathedral any longer'. The King of England threatened to convert to Islam if Alexander tried to force Becket's return on him. Whether Henry was serious is uncertain, though his education had included Arabic teachings newly arrived in Europe, and he admired Islamic scholars and art. When he built a new palace at Woodstock, it mirrored Sicilian buildings with Islamic influence, containing fountains and courtyards. The history of Western Europe might have been very different had Henry followed through with his threat.

Henry and Louis were moving closer to a peace arrangement by this time. In 1169, Henry met Louis at Montmirail to outline his plans for the succession, hoping to ease the French king's mind. Louis had the son he longed for, Philip, born to his third wife in 1165. Becket's constant interference was now causing Louis, and the Pope, problems. He was becoming a nuisance to everyone. On 14 June 1170, Henry arranged for the coronation of his son, who became known as Henry the Young King. The coronation of an heir during the ruling king's lifetime was an innovation of the French ruling family, the Capetians. It was a measure designed to counter the problems of an interregnum because there was already a crowned king in place when the old king died. The junior king gained no authority from the position, but there would be no succession crisis. The dynastic appeal to Henry II of importing this to England was clear.

The ceremony was conducted by the Archbishop of York in Becket's absence. Thomas was outraged. That may have been the intention. It brought him to the negotiating table as the French king and the Pope pressed for a final resolution to the dispute. It was agreed that Thomas would repeat the coronation of Henry the Young King alongside his wife, Louis's daughter. While Henry was in Normandy, Thomas crossed back to England for the first time in six years. Many of the English bishops gathered at Dover to welcome the Archbishop of Canterbury home. Thomas dodged

them, landed at Sandwich and rushed to Canterbury, where he set about excommunicating the king's supporters, including some bishops.

Henry was celebrating Christmas at his hunting lodge at Bur-le-Roi near Bayeux when news arrived of his former friend's latest antics. Henry's words became reported as 'Who will rid me of this turbulent priest?' The most contemporary record of his outburst is recorded in Latin by a monk at Canterbury who wrote about the incident. His words can be translated as 'What miserable drones and traitors have I nurtured and promoted in my household who let their lord be treated with such shameful contempt by a low-born cleric!' Whatever the words, Henry's intention has been debated from that day onwards. Did he mean it to be an instruction? Four knights rode from Bur-le-Roi to Canterbury Cathedral, bursting in with a small force on 29 December 1170. Their intention was to arrest Thomas, but when he resisted and taunted them the altercation became violent. The knights went outside, collected their swords and turned them on Thomas. The top of his skull was sliced off, causing his brains to spill on the cathedral floor.

At that moment, a new martyr was born. Thomas may have viewed this as his ultimate victory over Henry. Thomas Becket (the 'à' between his forename and surname is a Victorian addition) was canonised on 21 February 1173, just over two years after his death. St Thomas Becket would be England's premier saint until the Reformation. Henry's enemies made much of the terrible crime, blaming the king for murdering an archbishop in his cathedral. Henry led a campaign into Ireland, partly to absent himself for a while and partly to win favour with the Pope, bringing the Celtic Christians of Ireland under the control of the Roman Church. Eventually, after Henry swore on holy relics that he had not intended Becket's murder, the Pope forgave him.

Revolting Children

The next crisis of Henry's reign was a major revolt by his own sons. In January 1173, Henry the Young King fell out with his father over the lack of power he was being given. Henry II's inability to let go of power has been viewed as one of his weaknesses and as making the lashing out of his sons almost inevitable. However, Henry had made Richard, his second son, Duke of Aquitaine, with a degree of autonomy. His third son Geoffrey was Duke of Brittany. The fourth, John, was too young to be involved just yet. The problem lay with Henry the Young King. A celebrity on the tournament circuit, he appears to have lacked the qualities required in a ruler who would one day control vast and diverse territories. At least, that was what his father believed.

When Henry the Young King rebelled, his brothers Richard and Geoffrey joined him. Their revolt marked the realisation of Louis VII's strategy, which the Capetian king and his son would perfect. Henry II appeared all-powerful. His weakness was his sons. Stirring things up, Louis asked Young Henry why he had no power if he was a crowned king. Surely, Louis asked, old Henry had effectively retired when he had his son crowned. Louis knew well enough that this was not how junior kingship worked, having once held the office himself. Young Henry took the bait. He began to offer lands and money to anyone who would support him. William, King of Scotland was offered the

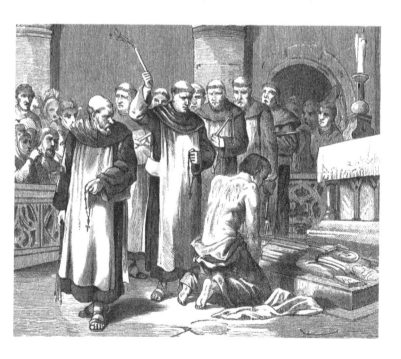

county of Northumberland. The Count of Flanders would get castles at Dover and Rochester, and, on top of this fire sale, Young Henry swore never to be reconciled with his father without the agreement of the King of France. He was demonstrating the very naivety that concerned his father.

In July 1174, Henry II landed in England to face down the revolt there. Instead of marching north from his landing point at Southampton, he moved west to Canterbury. When the cathedral came into sight, he dismounted, took off his boots and walked the remaining three miles barefoot. He arrived at the abbey, his feet cut and bleeding, and fell to his knees before Becket's shrine. He spent the night in prayer and insisted the monks of Canterbury whip him with wooden rods. On the morning of 12 July, he heard Mass in the cathedral before setting out for London. Once back in the capital, news quickly arrived that William, King of Scotland had been captured and imprisoned at Richmond Castle and the revolt had collapsed. It was positioned as having happened as Henry had been praying at Becket's shrine. What he had done in seeking forgiveness had been proven both necessary and successful. If Becket's martyrdom had been intended as a final victory over the king, Henry's harnessing of Becket's cult proved a last-minute comeback. God and St Thomas were back in Henry's corner.

LISTEN TO THE
PODCAST

Eleanor of Aquitaine

Eleanor, Henry's queen, was implicated in the revolt of their sons. One source claims she tried to reach Paris and her ex-husband's court to join her sons, riding in a man's clothes. Henry quickly forgave all those who rebelled against him, but Eleanor remained under a form of house arrest for the remainder of his life. Eleanor's part in the rebellion is hard to reconstruct from the available sources, which are almost universally hostile to her and to the majority of women with power. Her subsequent life in England was comfortable. She lived predominantly at Sarum Castle, one of her favourite homes, and was frequently at court when their children were present. As tragedy began to strike, Henry II and Eleanor seem to have turned to each other for comfort. There is a possibility that Eleanor took the blame for their sons' actions to allow their easy forgiveness and to prevent Louis from winning the game he had begun.

In the early 1180s, Young Henry and Geoffrey began to rebel again. One chronicler was quick to blame Geoffrey, whom he labelled 'that son of perdition', for leading his older brother astray, suggesting once more that Henry was unsuited to the role to which he had been born. Young Henry was reconciled to his father several times but fell back into revolt each time. After robbing two shrines in southern France, in what chroniclers saw as divine retribution, Young Henry was struck down with dysentery. The illness, which saw sufferers afflicted by violent diarrhoea, was common among campaigning armies in unsanitary conditions. King Henry's instinct was to rush to his son's side, but his advisers warned him against falling for what might be a trap. Instead, he sent a ring from his finger as a sign of his forgiveness to his son.

Young Henry understood the meaning of the ring. He was forgiven, but his father was not coming. He asked to be put in a hair shirt, a sign of piety. The constant itching and discomfort were designed to remind the wearer of Christ's suffering, their own sins and their need to behave well. He also had a noose placed round his neck. As his strength faded, he ordered his men to drag him from his bed using the noose and place him on a layer of ashes on the floor. They did as he asked, using a rock as a pillow. On 11 June 1183, aged 28, he died. When the news reached King Henry, he was utterly distraught. One witness noted, 'so great and so immoderate a grief oppressed the father, by a sorrow beyond all comparison deep, that, refusing all consolation, and perplexed between two evils, he declared that he had far rather that his son had triumphed over him than that death should have triumphed over his son'.

The Deaths of Kings

Louis VII died in 1180 and was succeeded by his son, Philip II, later known as Philip Augustus. Aged just 15 when he came to the throne, Philip had initially turned to Henry for support and advice, which had been freely given. Soon, though, the son would pick up his father's successful game with the sons of Henry II. He made a great fuss of Henry's third son Geoffrey, who was in Paris when he was killed in a tournament accident on 19 August 1186. Philip then turned his attention to Richard, the second son, and sought to divide him from his father.

In 1189 Henry was fleeing across France, chased by Philip and Richard, when he fell ill. A knight in his household, William Marshal, covered his escape at one point and almost killed Richard, sparing his life at the last moment. Philip and Richard burned Le Mans, Henry's birthplace and his favourite city, driving him out of there too. As the summer heat rose, Henry's health declined further. He arrived for peace talks so ill his men had to hold him in his saddle as he tried to grip onto consciousness. He agreed to all their terms, finally admitting defeat in his weakened state. As he gave his son the kiss of peace, Henry is reported to have whispered in Richard's ear, 'May the Lord never permit me to die until I have taken due vengeance upon you.'

As part of the deal, he was not permitted to extract oaths of loyalty from those rebels

LISTEN TO THE
PODCAST

The Medieval Origins
of the Coronation

who had backed Richard until one month before a planned crusading army departed. When he saw the name at the top of the list, he seemed to give in completely. It was John, his youngest and only other remaining son. A broken man, King Henry II died on 6 July 1189 at the age of 56.

Henry's career was remarkable, and he was perhaps the most gifted and successful person ever to sit on the throne of England or Great Britain. His sense of humour can be seen in his employment of Roland the Farter, who received land and an income for entertaining the king with 'one jump and whistle and one fart' each Christmas. He had been asked to become King of Jerusalem in 1185 but had declined, despite both the prestige and the family connection to the throne there. He knew what he was good at and played to his strengths.

The name Angevin, derived from his father's home, Anjou, is frequently applied to his lands and dynasty, though the term most closely associated with them is Plantagenet. Henry's father had a habit of wearing a sprig of broom plant as a badge. The Latin for broom plant is *planta genista*, which became Plantagenet. Rulers of that house would control England for the rest of the medieval period, a dynasty spanning 331 years and 14 kings.

Chapter 4

From Lionheart to Lamb of Rome

The Lionheart becomes king : The king's desire to go on crusade :
Richard's capture : The death of Richard I : King John and Arthur of
Brittany quarrel : The Archbishop of Canterbury dies : Disputes about
his successor : England suffers an interdict : John's unpopularity :
England is submitted to Rome

R ichard did not rush to England. He visited his father's body at Fontevrault Abbey. Entering in silence, he knelt in prayer beside the coffin, then got up and left to claim his inheritance. Chroniclers wrote that blood oozed from the corpse, a sure sign to the medieval mind that the murderer of the deceased was present. Richard was already Duke of Aquitaine but met Philip II to be invested as Duke of Normandy too, in return for a promise to marry Philip's sister Alix, who had been betrothed to Richard for years by this point, and to go on crusade with the French king.

In England, William Marshal, the knight who had almost killed Richard, arrived to tell Queen Eleanor the news of her husband's death, and that she was free. He found Eleanor at Winchester, already at liberty and aware of the news. She toured southern cities ensuring all remained calm until her son arrived. On 13 August 1189, Richard landed at Portsmouth. On the same day, his little brother John came ashore at Dover. Still, Richard did not hurry, apparently unconcerned about his brother's intentions as he created John Count of Mortain. The coronation of Richard I took place at Westminster Abbey on 3 September. He accepted the homage, the confirmation of their loyalty, from the bishops, earls and barons the following day, and then, according to one chronicler, 'put up for sale every thing he had'.

There was one overriding concern for Richard. His father had turned down the throne of Jerusalem, but Richard had a burning compulsion to go on a crusade. His upbringing in Aquitaine may have fed this desire – perhaps he felt the responsibility to family there more keenly than his father – and there was glory to be gained in the enterprise, too. He certainly felt no connection to England beyond a soft target to finance his crusade. Richard famously spent less than a year of his decade as King of England within his realm. His subjects may not have cared too much. They were used to an absent monarch, and a crusading one had strong public appeal. As long as the kingdom remained well ruled, Richard's lack of time in England would not be a problem.

On 2 July 1190, he met Philip at Vézelay. They travelled south through Italy, arriving in Sicily in September. Richard's sister was the former Queen of Sicily, and he found her imprisoned by her late husband's successor. He insisted on her release and forced the new king, Tancred, to come to terms, but this kept Richard tied up on the island until May 1191.

When the King of Cyprus tried to capture the ship containing Richard's sister and his bride-to-be, perhaps to ransom them, Richard turned his glare to another land. In a trademark over-reaction that showcased Richard's version of his father's incredible abilities, he swiftly conquered Cyprus and married Berengaria of Navarre there. Richard had extricated himself from his oath to marry Philip's sister Alix by claiming she had been Richard's father's mistress and had even given birth to Henry II's child. Reluctantly, Philip had consented, but the seeds of discord were sown.

Richard moved on to the Holy Land, where he led spectacular military victories that contributed to the emergence of his nickname, the Lionheart. He arrived at the Siege of Acre, and soon the city fell. He seemed unstoppable, to the annoyance of his senior allies like Philip, but was forced to make peace with his nemesis, Saladin, Sultan of Egypt and Syria, who proved a match for Richard.

LISTEN TO THE
PODCAST

Saladin and
the Crusades

England without a King

On 9 October 1192, Richard left the Holy Land to travel home. Philip had already left in July 1191, blaming poor health. Since arriving back in France, Philip had been snatching Richard's Continental lands and encouraging Richard's brother John into open revolt. This kind of activity was in direct contravention of the rules of crusading. A crusader's lands came under the Pope's protection while they were away and should not be attacked. Philip felt the opportunity was too good to miss, and the Pope was too weak to stop him. John needed little excuse to join in the endeavour in the hope of increasing his own power.

The structures Richard had put in place when he left England had worked incredibly well. King Stephen's captivity had demonstrated that the institution of the Crown could endure the absence of the one wearing it. The Chief Justiciar acted as regent in the king's absence, and the machinery of government was well evolved by Richard's reign.

Richard had also built alliances to help mitigate his absence. He had married Berengaria of Navarre in part to solidify a relationship with her father's kingdom, which lay on the western borders of Aquitaine – the part of his lands that Richard understood best. Philip encouraged uprisings there, but Sancho of Navarre, Berengaria's brother – 7'3" tall and a fearsome warrior – intervened to maintain peace. Philip tried to launch an assault

THE ROLE OF THE EXCHEQUER

Henry I is credited with introducing the Exchequer to receive and record income into the royal treasury. The Exchequer was an event that took place twice a year, at which money was submitted and checked against what was owed. Sheriffs were the king's representatives in the shires, and each year they would agree on the income due in taxation from their shire. They would attend the exchequer to submit the agreed amount. They would be responsible for any shortfall but could keep anything they raised over the agreed amount, which contributed to their reputation for greed and ruthlessness. The exchequer took its name from the chequered cloth that was spread over a board to help with the accounting process. This was recorded on tally sticks, which had notches cut in them to note the amounts paid or owed. Alongside this, a justiciar helped manage the running of the country while the king was gone.

on Normandy, but his barons refused to attack the lands of a crusader. Had Richard's absence been for the duration of the Third Crusade, as intended, his plans may have seen him return to a secure set of territories. Sadly for Richard, that was not to be.

During his time in the Holy Land, Richard had made enemies among his allies. When he was shipwrecked in the lands of the nephew of one of those enemies, he was arrested and sent to the court of Henry VI, the Holy Roman Emperor. Henry had agreed with Philip to detain Richard if he crossed his lands on his way home, despite the protection offered by his crusader status. He proved good to his word. Richard was held in captivity, and a vast ransom was set for his release. His mother, Eleanor, sprang into action, raising the ransom and delivering it herself to Germany to recover her son. Meanwhile, Philip and John made the most of Richard's unexpected and prolonged imprisonment. For his part, Richard charmed Henry, helping him resolve issues with his rebellious barons so that the Emperor grew to like and respect his prisoner. Philip and John began to plead with Henry to keep Richard imprisoned longer, even offering him money to delay the release when the ransom was on its way, but Henry refused. When Philip learned that Richard had been set free on 4 February 1194, he wrote to John, 'Look to yourself; the devil is loose.'

Richard was unable to spend time on England or other parts of his territories on his return, instead having to reclaim what Philip had snatched. During just over a year of captivity, John had been wrangling to take Richard's position, claiming at one point that his brother was dead. Meanwhile, Philip had been hacking away at the Angevin lands on the Continent. Richard thus began a prolonged series of military campaigns to regain what had been lost, in spite of the Pope's prohibition on attacking the lands of a crusader.

Richard was engaged all along the fringes of the Angevin lands. He made alliances against Philip with the counts of Flanders and Boulogne, as well as with his father-in-law Sancho VI, King of Navarre. In March 1199, the operations were still ongoing when Richard laid siege to the obscure castle of Châlus-Chabrol. It belonged to the Viscount of Limoges, who had rebelled in northern Aquitaine. While walking around the site on 26 March, Richard was hit in the shoulder by a crossbow bolt fired by an opportunistic defender on the walls. The wound turned gangrenous, and it soon became clear the king would not survive. The person who fired the bolt was brought before Richard.

LISTEN TO THE
PODCAST

Eleanor of Aquitaine

Most sources describe him as little more than a boy. He claimed he had lost his father and two brothers to Richard's forces, so the king ordered him forgiven and released. When the king died on 6 April 1199, his mother Eleanor of Aquitaine at his bedside, his men found the lad and flayed him alive, removing all of the skin from his body, before hanging him.

Richard had no legitimate children, only an illegitimate son named Philip of Cognac. There were two potential claimants to the throne. In Sicily, Richard indicated that his nephew, Arthur of Brittany, would be his heir. Arthur was the son of Geoffrey (the brother between Richard and John in age) and had been born after Geoffrey's death. The other candidate was John, who had been forgiven by Richard on his return from captivity and mentioned as heir since. However, succession was not a settled matter, and who held the stronger claim was wide open to debate. The issue was largely settled when the indomitable Eleanor of Aquitaine came out in favour of her youngest son, John. Arthur was only 12 years old, had been raised away from the family by Geoffrey's widow and was very close to King Philip, making his claim less appealing.

King John

John arrived at Chinon Castle too late for his brother's funeral but spent several days organising matters with his mother. He had caused trouble for Richard during his absence and was known as 'Lackland' because his father had left him no territory of his own. Suddenly, everything fell into John's lap. His suitability for the role must have been in doubt. William Marshal favoured John, but Hubert Walter, Archbishop of Canterbury and Chief Justiciar at Richard's death, preferred Arthur. Hubert perhaps knew John and his treachery better than some, but Eleanor had made her choice. *L'Histoire de Guillaume le Marechal* – The History of William Marshal, a biography written shortly after the knight's death – credits Hubert with prophetic words when he lost the argument. 'So be it then,' he conceded, 'but mark my words, Marshal, you will never regret anything in your life as much as this.'

With the succession decided, a prolonged interregnum was avoided. It fell to Hubert to crown the new king in a ceremony at Westminster Abbey on 27 May 1199, less than eight weeks after Richard's death. John found the Angevin lands diminished, partly by his efforts against Richard, and made peace with his

former ally Philip II of France, later known as Philip Augustus due to his expansion of Crown authority. Under the terms of the treaty, Philip would marry one of John's nieces, a princess of Castile. Eleanor made the journey to collect Blanche in 1200 and escorted her as far as Fontevrault on her way to be married. There, exhaustion seemed to prevent Eleanor from going any further.

Arthur of Brittany pressed his claims on the Continent as both John and Eleanor tried to resist the now 15-year-old. When Arthur besieged his grandmother Eleanor at Mirebeau Castle in 1202, John sped to her aid, successfully breaking the siege and capturing Arthur on 1 August 1202. Arthur's fate remains a mystery, but it is widely assumed he died in custody around the age of 16. Several chroniclers accuse John of personally murdering his nephew. *The Annals of Margam Abbey* record that 'when John was drunk he slew Arthur with his own hand and tying a heavy stone to the body cast it into the Seine'.

Almost immediately after becoming king, John set aside his wife of more than ten years, Isabella, Countess of Gloucester. In 1200, in his mid-thirties, John married the 14-year-old Isabella of Angoulême. She was already betrothed to someone else, but John wanted the alliance her marriage would bring for himself. This kind of behaviour had caused concern among John's subjects from the outset of his reign.

Hubert Walter was appointed Lord Chancellor despite his preference for Arthur at the succession, and became one of the greatest administrators in English history, credited with beginning to keep copies of royal documents. These include the Patent Rolls (records of letters issued 'patent', or unsealed, meant for public consumption), the Close Rolls (letters issued sealed for an individual or institution), Charter Rolls (recording the issue of royal charters and payments received for them), and Coroners' Rolls (records of inquests into sudden or unnatural deaths). John was also interested in administration, so it was perhaps the result of a shared concern, but Hubert's administrative structures would be used for generations.

The Battle of Mirebeau proved to be a rare high point for John's military efforts. Twenty-two of the prisoners captured there, in addition to Arthur, died from the poor treatment they received, alienating the local nobility. Spotting John's weakness, King Philip attacked Château Gaillard on the eastern border of Normandy. In 1203, John launched an unsuccessful counteroffensive. He withdrew and attacked Brittany to the west, attempting to lure Philip away, but this also failed. In December, John moved back to England and tried to set up a new defensive line on Normandy's eastern border. Philip simply moved south and swung under this line, giving him access to all of Normandy. In 1204, John's mother Eleanor of Aquitaine passed away, risking the remaining unity of the Angevin empire. By August 1204, Philip had taken Normandy, Anjou and Poitou, leaving John only parts of the Duchy of Aquitaine in his possession on the Continent.

On 13 July 1205 Hubert Walter, Archbishop of Canterbury, died. John visited Canterbury to assure the monks that they would be permitted to elect Hubert's successor freely but asked them to

delay the election. Replacing an Archbishop of Canterbury was a critical moment for the king and the kingdom. There had been a long-running rivalry with the archbishops of York, who claimed parity with Canterbury, but it was clear that Canterbury was being given precedence. As the senior clergyman and often a key member of the government, the appointment had far-reaching consequences. The

MONEY IN THE TIME OF KING JOHN

Almost all money at this stage was in the form of silver pennies. Pennies are often presented as d, which is an abbreviation of denarii, the Latin word for a penny. 12d made a shilling usually marked simply as s, and 20 shillings made a pound. £10, 5 shillings and 4 pence would usually be written as £10 5s 4d. A day's pay for an unskilled labourer was between 1d and 2d, or up to about £3 a year. More skilled workers may receive double that. A baron's income might be in the region of £600 a year. Senior nobles may be worth considerably more, highlighting the vast wealth gap.

relationship between the king and Archbishop of Canterbury could define the state of English politics for many years.

The right man in the role could act as the king's representative when the king was out of the kingdom without concern that he would become a rival to the king's power. The smooth interaction between Church and Crown at a time when both were at the centre of the kingdom's firmament was critical to a peaceful and prosperous realm. Many could still remember the damage done when Thomas Becket had fallen out spectacularly with John's father, Henry II. A king and archbishop at loggerheads was a recipe for disaster within the kingdom.

John sold the secular post of Lord Chancellor to Walter de Gray for 5,000 marks. A mark was a unit of currency equivalent to two-thirds of a pound – a vast amount for the time.

The Canterbury Controversy

Appointing a new archbishop was a more complex matter, involving three key stakeholders. The monks of Canterbury had a right to freely elect their preferred candidate as their archbishop. The king would also expect to be allowed some input because of the importance of the postholder in the realm. However, it was the Pope who had the right to invest the archbishop, to confirm him in the post officially, and the option to refuse to do so. Finding a candidate acceptable to all parties could therefore be tricky because their priorities were rarely aligned. John positioned his request for a delay as allowing time for careful contemplation by the monks. It may well have influenced him that the incomes from vacant sees, the areas overseen by bishops, went into the royal coffers. The monks of Canterbury agreed to the delay the king asked for. However, John's assurances that they would have the free election they were entitled to might have sounded hollow when he left, taking with him a valuable portable altar Hubert had left to the monks in his will.

Once the king had gone, the monks held an election. They chose their sub-prior Reginald and sent him as part of a delegation to Rome to have him invested by the Pope. John was outraged when he heard the news. He thundered into Christ Church, Canterbury on 11 December 1205 and chastised the monks, who immediately denied holding any election. John ordered them to immediately elect his chosen candidate, John de Gray, Bishop of Norwich, uncle of the new Chancellor and a close associate of the king. The terrified monks agreed, and John wrote to the Pope advising him that de Gray was the new Archbishop of Canterbury. Pope Innocent III was a relatively young Pope, elected in 1198 when he was around 38 years old. Under Innocent, the papacy became more robust and sought to unify Christian Europe by

asserting Rome's authority over aspects of secular life and rule. Faced with the dilemma of two competing candidates for the archbishopric of Canterbury, one favoured by the monks and the other by the king, the Pope sought, and found, the opportunity the crisis presented.

Innocent selected an alternative candidate: Stephen Langton, an Englishman who was a cardinal in Rome. What the monks of Canterbury thought is not recorded, but John's reaction is well known. The Pope's interference in his kingdom was bad enough, especially when John had sent Innocent a perfectly good candidate he claimed had been elected by the monks. John refused to recognise the Pope's choice, and eventually, in 1207, Pope Innocent invested Stephen Langton against the king's wishes. The fact that Langton, as part of the Parisian intellectual movement, came from the same educational background as Thomas Becket must have rung alarm bells. What Innocent overlooked, or failed to care sufficiently about, was the damage a confrontation between king and archbishop was likely to generate. When that king was as belligerent, petty and failing as John was, it was a super-heated melting pot. John took into royal hands all of the lands and incomes of the archbishopric of Canterbury and refused to allow Langton to enter England.

John's first legitimate child was born when the king was at the relatively late age of 40. On 1 October 1207, Isabella of Angoulême was delivered of a son and heir for the king who was named Henry. Six months later, the good news of a secured succession (subject to the uncertainties of child mortality) was shaken by the spiralling of relations with Rome. England was placed under an interdict.

It is hard to overestimate the impact of this measure on everyday life in England at that time. An interdict meant the withdrawal of religious services. With the exception of care for the dying and a few feast days, the Church shut up its doors. There were no baptisms, which risked the eternal souls of precarious new lives. Weddings could not be celebrated, and funerals, as well as burials on consecrated ground, were prohibited. The church bells that punctuated the day with reassuring regularity fell silent. No English subject's soul was being ministered to or cared for, which placed everyone at risk of a prolonged stay in purgatory or worse. It was spiritually disastrous for every person

WHAT IS AN INTERDICT?

An interdict was a punishment available under the Catholic Church's rules, known as canon law. It is still provided for today under the 1983 Code of Canon Law. A person affected by an interdict is forbidden to participate in church services or receive their spiritual benefit. If a place is under interdict, all church services there are withdrawn.

in the kingdom. At a time when religion was at the very core of everyday life in England, this was designed to terrify John's subjects and turn them against him in the hope that doing so would force the king to back down.

King John, at least, was able to offset that damage with the thought that he was about to become more wealthy than he, or any other king of England, had ever been. The early years of Henry II's reign had seen royal revenues passing through the Exchequer of around £13,000 per year. By the later years of his rule, in the 1180s, that income had climbed to the region of £22,000 a year. Access to the wealth of the Church and the Crown made John incredibly rich very quickly. For the first time in more than a century, England had a king with nowhere else to go and nowhere else to worry about but England. That scrutiny was painful, as John used the administration his father had installed and his brother had refined to squeeze more and more money from every corner. He was concerned primarily with building a war chest to finance a renewed effort to take back what he believed was his on the Continent.

England's Soul Is Lost

In October 1209, Stephen Langton, who by now had been Archbishop of Canterbury for three years but was still barred from England, excommunicated King John. Excommunication is another sanction available to the Church to punish those it believes are committing crimes against canon law. The measure removes the excommunicated from the community of the Church, withdrawing access to all religious services and therefore the hope of salvation. Although it was frequently overused in medieval Europe, it was designed to be the ultimate sanction to correct behaviour. With the interdict still in place and the King of

England excommunicated, all but one of the bishops of England left.

As the people and the nobility worried increasingly about their immortal souls, which now had almost no chance of the salvation required to leave purgatory and enter Heaven, John began to enjoy the situation. All of the income of the Church in England fell into the open, hungry royal coffers. What had been the Church's wealth became John's wealth, and what had previously been sent to Rome remained firmly in John's bulging cash reserves. John used every trick in the book, and plenty from outside it, to gather more and more money. His income at the Exchequer was estimated at £30,000, without taking into account other income, which far exceeded what his brother or father had achieved. Confiscating the property of nobles, taxing the Jewish population and charging for things like permission to marry made John richer but increasingly unpopular. The king was blinded to the problems he was storing up by the glint of the silver coins that surrounded him.

The increasing extent of John's ruthlessness towards his barons was demonstrated terrifyingly in 1210. It was also a turning point in John's relations with his nobility and the suspicion they viewed the king with.

William de Braose had been at Richard I's deathbed and had been given custody of Arthur, Duke of Brittany before his disappearance. Precisely why John turned on William is unclear, though some sources point to an ill-advised comment by William's wife Maud that they should not trust John with their children given what he did to Arthur. The official reason seems to have been the non-payment of debts. William was hunted by John, moving through Ireland and Wales and eventually being forced to flee to France, where he died the following year. Maud and the couple's oldest son William were taken captive, and the extortionate sum of £40,000 was demanded for their release. De Braose being either unwilling or more likely unable to pay such a sum, they remained in prison until John gave instructions that they were no longer to be given food or water. When their cell was eventually opened, it was reported that they were found dead, huddled together, Maud's teeth marks scarring young William's cheek. She had been driven to try to eat her own son's flesh to stay alive. John's malice, untrustworthiness and fickle nature were being laid bare to his barons at every turn.

William Marshal also fell under John's increasingly paranoid suspicion. Marshal had assisted de Braose, a fellow landowner in Ireland, when he sought safe haven. When de Braose rebelled, Marshal abandoned him and joined John on the campaign against de Braose in Wales. Despite this, John turned on Marshal, demanding that he answer for harbouring de Braose. Marshal coolly offered to undergo trial by combat to prove his innocence and his loyalty. However much John cast around, he could find no champion willing to take on the famous William Marshal and was forced to let the matter drop. Alive and free, but shaken, Marshal, by now in his mid-sixties, retired to his Irish lands to escape John's unpredictable wrath.

Military action in Ireland and Wales in the wake of William de Braose's revolt had seen John assert his dominance there, and in 1209 he had bullied the elderly William I, the Lion, King of Scots, who was by now almost 70 years old, into recognising once again the fealty he had conceded to Henry II. Alongside that, Scotland was required to pay £10,000 to the English Crown. All of this heavy-handed treatment of his subjects, along with the interdict and excommunication that meant the population became dangerously disconnected from their spiritual anchor points as the king grew richer, left John with a problem. In all parts of his kingdom, the walls of treasure rooms creaked and groaned under the weight of the coin John had accumulated. John had chests and barrels bursting with silver pennies, which were heavy and difficult to move around. What was he going to do with all this unprecedented accumulated wealth?

Regaining the Angevin Empire

There was little debate and no doubt in John's mind. He had lost most of his Continental holdings by 1204 and felt that he was now in a position to attempt to recover them. He put the money he had gathered to work. In the spring of 1212, John focussed his attention across the Channel. Philip's success in imposing direct Crown control on parts of France that had previously only owed a loose, nominal fealty to Paris left many of his nobles feeling uncomfortably constricted. This was the chink in Philip's armour that John, with his freeing wealth, could exploit at will. He began to build an alliance against Philip and ordered a muster of his English forces at Portsmouth. However well-prepared John was, and however much money he was able to throw at his plans, he was about to discover that he could not control everything. With his arrangements progressing nicely, disturbing and aggravating news of a fresh uprising in Wales led by Llywelyn ap Iorwerth reached the king. He was forced to divert his army to quash this revolt and so abandon plans to invade France.

Meanwhile, Pope Innocent III stepped up his campaign against the King of England. He must have been frustrated that John was so unfazed by the withdrawal of Church services from England and his personal excommunication and was in fact profiting as he raked in more and more cash that should have gone to the Church. In 1212, Innocent issued a papal bull reiterating John's excommunication and declaring him dethroned.

England's barons were free to select their own replacement for John. Even with his vast reserves of cash – or perhaps because of them – this was uncomfortable for John. The Pope had declared

FROM LIONHEART TO LAMB OF ROME

WHAT IS A PAPAL BULL?

A papal bull is a public decree from the Pope. Like letters patent, they are issued open, for public consumption. Popes could use them to call for crusades, settle disputes and endorse bodies such as the Knights Templar.

open season on his vastly wealthy Crown. The feeling must have intensified when a brave hermit, Peter of Wakefield, made public a prophecy of the king's death.

Before the end of the summer of 1212, Peter's words were looking dangerously close to coming true. A plot was exposed to murder John, led by two of his barons, Eustace de Vesci and Robert Fitzwalter. The cause of their disaffection is unclear, beyond John's constant squeezing of the realm and his barons and the fresh encouragement from Innocent to do something about it. Whether the stories that John had seduced de Vesci's wife and Fitzwalter's daughter were true – and John was renowned for precisely this type of thing – is hard to be certain of. What brought these two men together is also unclear. De Vesci was a northern landowner, and Fitzwalter was a southerner with close ties to the king. The lack of a single incident conclusively binding them together is perhaps symptomatic of a more general and widespread dissatisfaction with, or fear of, John about which the Pope had now equipped them, even compelled them, to do something. The plot was exposed, and de Vesci and Fitzwalter fled abroad, taking care to extract their families.

Shaken by the threat to his Crown, John set about planning for the spring. As the weather warmed, it became clear Philip was preparing to reverse John's plans. The French king had tasked his son and heir Louis, the Lion, with an invasion of England and the dethronement of John, something that now took on the air of a holy crusade. As tensions mounted and John's paranoia and mistreatment of his barons left him feeling intensely the isolation and vulnerability that had stalked him for years, John took the astonishing step of giving away his kingdom. So unexpected and effective was it that it remains hard to tell whether it was a stroke of diplomatic genius or the last resort of a desperate man. John sent word to the Pope, and Innocent III rushed to grasp the shocking offer.

On 15 May 1213, John had a meeting with Pandulf, a papal legate, a representative delegated to wield the power of the Pope. The offer was so surprising that John wrote it down in a letter to be delivered to Innocent to ensure that what he was offering was clear and unambiguous. No doubt Innocent wanted the reassurance of the king's word in writing too to avoid future withdrawal, denial or interpretation of it. John wrote that the decision had been taken because 'we have grieved and offended God and our

mother church of Rome, and forasmuch as we have need to the mercy of our lord Jesus Christ'. John went on to explain his offer to Innocent.

We offer and freely grant to God, and to the apostles of St Peter and Saint Paul, and to our mother church of Rome, and to our Holy father the Pope, Innocent the third, and to all the Popes that cometh after him, all the realm and patronages of churches of England and of Ireland, with all the appurtenances, for remission of our sins, and help of our kin's souls, and of all Christian souls, so that, from this time afterward, we will receive and hold of our mother church of Rome, as fee farm, doing fealty to our holy father the Pope, Innocent the third, and to all the Popes that cometh after him, in manner abovesaid.

John clarified the effect of this submission to Rome by adding that it would 'bind us, and all that cometh after us, and our heirs forevermore, without any gainsaying, to the Pope'. After all of the disputes and bloodshed over papal interference in England and the resistance to a Pope having a say in matters the king deemed his alone to judge, John gifted the kingdom to the papacy. Innocent III became the liege lord of England. After 150 years of his predecessors finding ways to avoid bending the knee to the King of France to offer fealty for his lands across the Channel, John offered to do just that to the Pope for the Crown of England. For Innocent, a Pope devoted to expanding papal authority and unifying Christian Europe into a crusading powerhouse, the appeal was plain to see. Not only did he end a prolonged and utterly ineffective attempt to punish a Christian king and his realm, but he now had a model to demonstrate how a kingdom ruled by Rome could function for the benefit of all Christendom. A model others might follow.

For John, the move meant a spectacular volte-face and the

surrender of all his royal authority, so jealously guarded for 14 years. He must have felt the loss was worth what he gained. Immediately, John was transformed from an international pariah to the darling of the papacy. He would pay Rome an annual tribute of 1,000 marks (£666), but then he could afford that easily. Archbishop Langton was finally allowed to travel to England. It remained to be seen how much day-to-day interference he might have to endure but, in an instant, the Pope forbade Philip and Louis's plans to launch a crusading invasion of England. England enjoyed special protection, and John became the Pope's feted prodigal son. This was a monumental moment in English history. The King of England was, voluntarily, no longer the master within the bounds of his own kingdom. John tied himself and all of his successors to the Pope and his successors in Rome. Technically, this link remained unbroken until Henry VIII severed England's links with the Roman Church and declared himself Supreme Head and Sole Protector of the Church in England in 1531.

However, if John felt he had defused matters in 1213, whether by a clever tactical manoeuvre or in an act of desperation that appeared to resolve his troubles, he was to be proven wrong. The gifting of England to the papacy had long-lasting impacts on the kingdom, but John would feel the pressure almost immediately. Although he had swiftly and effectively removed the threat of foreign invasion, he had not improved relations with his own barons. The further deterioration of the situation within England would tear the kingdom apart and lead to one of English history's defining moments.

Chapter 5

Angevin Dreams

The Battle of Bouvines : England's barons rebel : Magna Carta :
John's young son becomes King Henry III : The Battle of Lincoln :
Establishing the Great Charter : The birth of Parliament : Henry's
peace : The Provisions of Oxford : Simon de Montfort's Rebellion :
The Battle of Lewes : King Henry is captured

When King John marched north with his army from the slumbering coastal villages and balmy fields of Aquitaine in the summer of 1214, it had seemed like a well-laid and lavishly financed plan. In the preceding months, John had been using his vast reserves of money to buy alliances against the French king. He paid the barons of Flanders to cause trouble while he assembled a fleet and an army. John then sailed to Poitou in Aquitaine, where he gathered more support from barons disaffected with King Philip of France. As he marched north, his allies, led by his nephew Otto, the Holy Roman Emperor and including the Duke of Brabant, the counts of Flanders and Boulogne, as well as John's illegitimate half-brother William Longespée, Earl of Salisbury, moved south. Their aim was to catch Philip in a pincer movement.

Whether because John was personally uninspiring and often offensive or because they simply thought better of rebellion, the barons of Poitou abandoned John and went home. The king was forced to sit on his hands and hope Otto and his other allies in the north could succeed without him. On 27 July 1214, Philip met his enemies. Pitched battles were still a rarity in an age that favoured the predictability and relative safety of siege warfare. All John could do was wait for news. When it came, the tidings were dreadful. Otto had fled. Salisbury and the counts of Boulogne and Flanders were captured. Some sources gave the total number of prisoners taken as around 9,000. One chronicler, known only as the Anonymous of Béthune, considered Philip's victory so complete that, from then on, 'no one dared wage war against him'. Battles were decided by God's judgement. God was still not on his side for all John's plans, money and backing from Rome.

When John returned to England with his tail between his legs, he was met by disgruntled barons, particularly those from the north. All of his cruel and extreme extractions had not brought victory. Now, they demanded reform. John was faced by armed men in London in January 1215 at a conference but was in no mood to appease them. He began hiring mercenaries to build his own army, clearly expecting to have to defend his Crown at home. John also sought to reinforce his protection from Rome by taking the crusader's oath, though it is doubtful he ever meant to go through with it. Yet by early spring 1215 it became clear that the king's manoeuvring was not working. A document named the Unknown Charter was circulating, which harked back to Henry I's coronation charter. It may have been part of the negotiations the barons had sought to begin in January, and over the following months it would evolve into a document that would define John's reign and English politics for centuries.

Aware of John's suspicion, which might have been paranoia but for the fact that he was right, the barons began to use the tournament circuit as a cover for their meetings. On 5 May 1215, at a

THE TOURNAMENT CIRCUIT

Medieval tournaments began as sprawling war games, with the aim of capturing rival knights. Doing so would entitle the captor to keep their horse or claim a ransom, and the circuit made some knights, such as Sir William Marshal, incredibly rich. The events could cover miles of countryside or drive through towns, involving hundreds of contestants. It was only later in the medieval period when tournaments evolved into the more contained jousting contests associated with the Tudor period.

Nobilium virorum Willmi Marescalli Comitis Penbroke, Willmi Comitis Sar, Willmi Comitis Waren, Willmi Comitis Arundell, Alani de Galloeya Constabularii Scotie, Warini filii Geroldi, Petri filii Hereberti. Huberti de Burgo Senescalli Pictavie, Hugonis de Nevill, Mathei filii Herberti, Thome Basset, Alani Basset, Philippi de Albini, Roberti de Roppeleia, Johis Marescalli, Johis filii Hugonis, 7 aliorum fidelium nostrorum:

tournament in Northamptonshire, a group of barons renounced their fealty to John. Fealty was an oath that recognised the feudal overlordship of another. Breaking fealty was treason. Renouncing it avoided accusations of treason but meant giving up all land and titles held from the king. John offered to help resolve the dispute, but only in his courts, which would only ever favour him. When the barons refused, John began laying siege to their castles. War in England had begun.

London fell quickly to the rebels, as many in the mercantile city shared their concerns. This forced John to the negotiating table. Intensive talks took place in late May and early June to find peace. The Unknown Charter was evolving. One of its incarnations survives as The Articles of the Barons. It is easy to imagine each paragraph, sentence, and then word being painstakingly examined and refined. On Monday 15 June, the talks were completed. The barons met with the king at Runnymede, partway between his base at Windsor and theirs in London. Here, the peace treaty now known as Magna Carta (the Great Charter) was offered to the barons by the king. It contained 63 clauses concerned with the governance of the realm and the settlement of disputes between the Crown and the barons. Four copies of the 1215 Charter survive. Two rest at the British Library, one at Salisbury Cathedral and one at Lincoln Castle. Three clauses remain on the statute books of the United Kingdom today. One guarantees the freedoms of the English Church, one confirms the liberties of the City of London, but perhaps the most famous are Clauses 39 and 40 of the 1215 Charter, which were later brought together. This provision ensures a right to due process under law, stating:

No Freeman shall be taken or imprisoned, or be disseised of his Freehold, or Liberties, or free Customs, or be outlawed, or exiled, or any other wise destroyed; nor will We not pass upon him, nor condemn him, but by lawful judgment of his Peers, or by the Law of the land. We will sell to no man, we will not deny or defer to any man either Justice or Right.

After four days of consideration, most of the barons accepted the treaty, reaffirming their fealty to John. Some, particularly northern barons, refused to trust in John's offer and stormed home. They were proven right. Within six weeks, John had appealed to Pope Innocent III as his liege lord and was instructed to destroy the Charter. The papal bull issued on 24 August made it clear that anyone seeking to rely on the Charter would be

LISTEN TO THE
PODCAST

Magna Carta

excommunicated. Innocent described the document as 'illegal, unjust, harmful to royal rights and shameful to the English people'. John relied on the fact that it also impacted Innocent's rights as the feudal overlord of England. War had seemed a threat that had passed, but it now returned with a vengeance.

Despite its later reputation, Magna Carta was initially a complete failure and a catalyst for a civil war known as the First Barons' War. In response, the Brut Chronicle explains that the barons 'ordained among them the best speakers and wisest men, and sent them over the sea to King Philip of France'. They asked Philip to send his son and heir, Louis the Lion, to invade England. In return, they would welcome Louis as their new king and help him drive John out. On 22 May 1216, Louis landed at Sandwich in Kent. John moved to Corfe Castle in Dorset as Louis and the barons swept to take control of swathes of the kingdom. John gathered those who remained loyal and all of his treasure and marched north along the Welsh Marches before cutting east, trying to put out the fires of rebellion wherever he could. Yet catastrophe struck. On 12 October 1216, John was taking a dangerous shortcut across the Wash, between Lincolnshire and Norfolk, when his baggage train was caught in the incoming tide. His money, holy relics and, according to some accounts, his crown slipped beneath the water and into the thick mud.

As the stress of what he had brought on himself gripped the king, he succumbed to illness, possibly dysentery. A frequent problem for campaigning armies, for which cleanliness was difficult, dysentery resulted in what was frequently described as the stomach turning to water. Those afflicted suffered violent diarrhoea that caused dehydration and was often fatal. John had to be carried on a litter as his health declined. On 18 October 1216 at Newark Castle, John slipped from life as his kingdom slid from Angevin control.

The Greatest Knight

At this time, the French king Louis 'the Lion' was in control of most of the southwest of England, with his allies in the north extending his influence there. But John had left behind a will, a tiny document held at Worcester Cathedral where he is buried. In it, he hoped those named at the end, 13 of his most powerful remaining allies, would do all they could to help his son come to the Crown. Among those listed was William Marshal, a man who would lead the effort to retake England. In his late sixties, the man remembered as 'The Greatest Knight' was about to embark on his most challenging endeavour. Although he expressed his reservations, Marshal eventually accepted the post of regent for John's oldest son, the eight-year-old Henry. When Marshal met the boy, he vowed, 'I will be yours in good faith and there is nothing I will not do to serve you while I have the strength'.

Together, they rode to Gloucester, where Marshal had determined to have Henry crowned King Henry III. For all his successes, Louis was slow to arrange a coronation. Marshal saw the chance to steal a march and have his candidate anointed first. On 28 October 1216, ten days after his father's death, Henry was crowned in a makeshift ceremony at Gloucester Cathedral. The papal legate Guala's presence helped reinforce Henry's investiture's legitimacy. On 11 November in Bristol, Marshal was officially appointed guardian of the king and realm. One of his first acts was a stroke of genius. He reissued Magna Carta, disavowed by John, with Guala's support. The document was largely the same as that of 1215. The most contentious element, which allowed the barons to take control of the government if they considered the king was behaving badly, was dropped, but most other provisions remained.

In a moment, all of the barons in open rebellion because of the scrapping of Magna Carta found their reason for revolt removed. Barons began to return. They were known in royal records as the *reversi*, but they were initially few, and slow to come. Yet Marshal knew that there could be no lasting peace while Louis remained in England. In late February 1217, Louis went to France to seek his father's help. By the time he returned in April, Marshal had been busy hoovering up castles and ports in the south. Though he soon abandoned them, lacking the resources to defend them properly, he had succeeded in twisting the lion's tail.

When Marshal heard that the remaining northern rebel barons were attacking Lincoln Castle and that Louis's men were moving to join them, he saw a chance to do what Robert, Earl of Gloucester had done to Stephen in 1141: corner his enemy in Lincoln. The Crown's enemies were gathering in Lincoln, where Nicholaa de la Haye held the castle as England's first female sheriff. Under her leadership, the castle had been holding out for at least three months before Marshal's relief army arrived.

On 20 May 1217, a second critical battle in less than a century took place at Lincoln. Some crossbowmen were let into a postern

NICHOLAA DE LA HAYE, SAVIOUR OF THE KINGDOM

In a period when the liberty of women was generally limited, Nicholaa de la Haye is remarkable for having inherited the position of Constable of Lincoln Castle and twice defended it from attacking French and rebel English forces. Nicholaa had been made Sheriff of Lincolnshire by King John in 1216 and remained a resolute supporter of King Henry III. Her defence of the castle in allegiance with Henry proved a turning point during the First Barons' War.

gate in the castle, a hidden entrance that could be used during a siege. As they shot at the forces gathered between the castle and cathedral, Marshal assaulted the town's north gate. Now 70 years old, Marshal was so keen to engage that a squire had to grab the reins of his horse and remind him to put his helmet on. Marshal's biography would boast that a 'hungry lion never rushed on its prey so hotly as the Marshal on his foes'.

The commander of Louis's forces was the Count of Perche. When a spear caught the count's helmeted head, Marshal jumped down from his own horse to take the reins of the count's, fearing his foe was injured. The count smashed his sword into the top of Marshal's helmet, denting the protection he almost had not worn. But then the count fell from his saddle – the spear wound had proven fatal after all. It was shocking for a senior nobleman to be killed in battle. While men-at-arms might be targeted and shown no mercy, noblemen expected to be captured for ransom. The death of the Count of Perche, therefore, shocked everyone. The French forces panicked and fled. The royal forces had won a stunning military victory, and Marshal's gamble had paid off.

Louis made one last bid to rejuvenate his cause. He allied with Eustace the Monk, a pirate who had seized control of the Channel Islands in 1205. Their fleet was met by an English one under the command of Hubert de Burgh, the justiciar. Marshal had reportedly wanted to lead the attack but had been prevented by those concerned for his safety.

On 24 August 1217, the fleets met at the Battle of Sandwich. The English left port with the tide and the wind against them. As Hubert's ship drew near the French fleet, he suddenly veered off course and sped up. The French taunted the cowardly English as they appeared to flee. However, with the wind behind them, the English drew

LISTEN TO THE
PODCAST

Nicholaa de la Haye

alongside the French ships and began to throw powdered lime into the air. It was a form of chemical warfare. Lime was used in buildings to make mortar, but it was a dangerous substance. It was caustic and burned on contact with water. As it got into French sailors' eyes, mouths and other sweaty areas, it seared their skin and eyeballs. Blinded, the French were subjected to crossbow volleys and were rammed by the iron-clad prows of the English ships. The victory was so complete that only 15 of the French fleet of 80 ships made it home. Eustace the Monk was found hiding below deck on his flagship and was executed. In the aftermath, Louis was forced to accept peace and leave England.

Rebalancing Power

Henry III's coronation was repeated at Westminster Abbey on 17 May 1220, just to make sure that it was entirely legitimate. England was faced with many years of a minority government under Henry III. There was still dissatisfaction and mistrust to be put right. Magna Carta was reissued again in 1217. An additional document, the Charter of the Forest, separated out some provisions that dealt with royal forest lands, leaving Magna Carta to deal with the remaining issues. It is in comparison to the smaller Charter of the Forest that Magna Carta was given its name. It would be reissued again in 1225.

The Charter became part of a rebalancing of power in England. It established that the monarch was not above the laws of the land, and, increasingly, taxation was used as a carrot to encourage the king to correct perceived deviations from the requirements of Magna Carta.

It was during the reign of Henry III that Parliament emerged as a body to add to the governmental structures of medieval England. The word first appears in use in 1236 to describe

TAXES

Taxation took the form of a percentage tax on moveable property, which was essentially anything except a house or other building. Those in the countryside would pay one-fifteenth of the value of their moveable goods, while those in towns would be required to pay one-tenth. This taxation was irregular for one-off projects but came on top of tithes. Tithes were taxes due to the Church and were often paid in produce.

what would previously have been a Great Council. The job of Parliament in its first iteration was to grant taxation to the Crown for war or special projects. In return for grants of taxation, the king would be required to amend his behaviour in identified ways that breached his obligations under Magna Carta. By 1254, elected Members of Parliament were attending sessions. They were knights from the shires representing their local area, and it is possible some towns also provided members.

Parliament would develop further as a result of the biggest political crisis of Henry III's reign. Henry is often a forgotten monarch, despite ruling for 56 years. His reign was also the longest of any English medieval monarch and would only be exceeded by that of George III in the early 19th century. Following the problems of Richard's reign and the disasters of John's, and ruling for as long as he did, it is unsurprising that Henry faced significant issues. He married Eleanor of Provence, several of whose family came to England. Originating from around Savoy, they were known as the Savoyards. They became increasingly unpopular as Henry gave them titles, lands and offices in England, while barons despised the influence of foreign favourites at their own expense. Papal control of England caused trouble when representatives from Rome periodically arrived to extract money, usually for crusading efforts. There seemed to be a view on the Continent that England was bulging with cash and ripe for the plucking, an idea perhaps created by John's hoarding.

When he came of age, Henry initially sought to resurrect his father's plans to regain control of the Angevin continental lands. On 30 April 1230, he set sail from Portsmouth. He enjoyed early success, with Brittany and Poitou quickly secured. When both Henry and his younger brother Richard fell seriously ill, they were forced to abandon the campaign, and by October they were back in England. It would be 12 years before Henry was able to try again. He declared war on King Louis IX, the son of Louis the Lion, on 8 June 1242. He enjoyed initial success in Poitou and Gascony, parts of Aquitaine. Louis retaliated with lightning speed. At Taillebourg, the two armies lined up on opposite banks of the Charente River. Convinced by his brother Richard that they could not win, Henry withdrew to Saintonge. Louis pursued the English army, but they fought an inconclusive battle in which one English chronicler claimed that the French 'were forced to confess that the English gained the most honour'.

Louis's army continued to grow and pressed Henry further and further back, the English king giving alms (donations to the poor) at every stop. This seemed to generate some sympathy for the English king, who many viewed as a preferable lord to Louis. Those towns hid their food supplies and poisoned their own wells as the French army approached. As many as 80 French nobles lost their lives to this tactic, as well as up to 20,000 French soldiers. When Louis himself fell ill, his advisers panicked and encouraged their king to seek a truce.

A cold war would continue until the Treaty of Paris was agreed on 4 December 1259. Under the terms of the agreement, Henry acknowledged the permanent loss of Normandy, Maine, Touraine

Alexander Rey Scotore / lewellin princeps wallie

PARLIAMENT
OF EDWARD I.

and the Angevin patrimony in Anjou. He would remain Duke of Aquitaine with control of Gascony, a smaller area than the duchy, but only as a vassal of the French Crown. The chronicler Matthew of Westminster believed the agreement was a relief to Henry because the 'prodigal anxiety of the King of England was released from its burdens'. He was no longer compelled to pursue a lost cause in the name of a vanished honour.

Unprecedented Peace

Henry and Louis were remarkably similar characters. Both were deeply pious, though Louis was more militarily minded. He had been on a crusade in the Holy Land and would become a saint, something Henry would surely have dearly loved for himself. After a century of conflict with the Capetian kings of France, Henry and Louis now enjoyed a period of unprecedented peace. France was not the only place in which Henry would secure long periods of concord. Henry's oldest daughter, Margaret, born in 1240, was married to Alexander III, King of Scots in 1251. This created a uniquely close bond between the royal families, who were keen to spend time in each other's company. In turn, peace between the kingdoms was promoted. In Wales, Henry agreed the Treaty of Montgomery in September 1267. He recognised Llywelyn ap Gruffudd, ruler of Gwynedd, as Prince of Wales, the only time an English monarch acknowledged a native Welsh ruler in this way.

Despite this wide-ranging peace and concord with foreign powers, or perhaps because of it, Henry is considered a bit of a failure as a king. There is still a temptation to view those who stomp around other kingdoms of Europe trying to conquer them as good medieval monarchs, which is odd when we would not expect our leaders to behave that way today. Henry did not fit that mould, and part of his problem was that he never quite managed to fit the other model of medieval kingship either. A ruler was expected to be a powerful military leader or wise figure. Henry was neither. His military campaigns failed. He was very pious and venerated Edward the Confessor, who was deemed to fall into the wise ruler category, but Henry made mistakes that betrayed his lack of wisdom.

Significant among his errors of judgement is the Sicilian

Affair of the 1250s. In 1252, Pope Innocent IV wrote to offer Henry the throne of Sicily. More accurately, he offered to sell the Crown to Henry. Innocent had fallen out with King Conrad and was looking for an alternative. The Pope had already offered the kingdom to the Count of Anjou and even to Henry's own brother, Richard of Cornwall. Richard had laughed it off, saying, 'You may as well say: I will sell or give you the moon; now climb up and take it.' To his brother's horror, Henry enthusiastically grasped the scheme, deciding to get the Crown of Sicily for his younger son, Edmund. What Innocent offered to sell was only, in fact, the right to lay claim to Sicily. Henry would then have to raise an army, take it into the Mediterranean and win the island himself. It proved a prolonged, deeply embarrassing episode for Henry. Everyone knew it was an impossible dream, except Henry himself. The affair demonstrated his political naivety and lack of wisdom that prevented him from falling into that category of good kings.

The winter of 1257–8 was bitter. England was gripped by famine. One chronicler recorded that 'The dead lay about, swollen and rotting, on dunghills, and in the dirt of the streets,

FOREIGN FAVOURITES

The Poitevins, a group of foreign favourites centred around Henry's half-siblings, were expelled from England by the council. Henry's mother, Isabella of Angoulême, had remarried after King John's death. Her second husband was Hugh X de Lusignan. Subsequently one of Henry's half-brothers became Bishop of Winchester, another became Earl of Pembroke, and a half-sister became Countess of Surrey. It was the kind of preferential treatment of foreigners that often provoked a backlash.

and there was scarcely anyone to bury them.' It proved to be a portent of trouble. In April 1258, a group of barons in armour confronted Henry in his chamber. They had left their weapons outside, and, when the king asked whether he was their prisoner, they assured him he was not. Yet. The Sicilian Affair and favouritism consistently displayed to the queen's family were causing growing frustration. The delegation was similar to that which had tried to convince John to reform his ways. It was looking dangerously like history was repeating itself.

In June, negotiations took place in Parliament at Oxford to try to diffuse the growing tension. The result was a document known as the Provisions of Oxford. The most controversial part of the compromise was the establishment of a panel of 24 barons to act as a check on the king's power. This had been a provision within Magna Carta, too, but had contributed to its failure and had been omitted when William Marshal reissued it. The original plan allowed for the baronial council to declare war on the king if it felt such a step was necessary, opening the door to civil war. The new body did not have that authority but was positioned as a support mechanism to help Henry make better decisions.

It was still a curtailment of royal authority that would be hard for a king to endure. One of the first actions of the panel was to declare 'that there are to be three parliaments a year'. The 24 had the right to attend whether they were specifically summoned or not. Although it still gathered in the king's name at his desire, for the first time the summoning and composition of Parliament was removed from the king's hands in practical terms.

Thunder and Lightning

In July, Henry was on a barge on the Thames when a thunderous storm erupted overhead. Frightened, he ordered the barge to pull in at the nearest wharf, where he disembarked and scurried into the Bishop of Durham's palace. The palace was occupied at that moment by Simon de Montfort, Earl of Leicester. Simon was

Henry's brother-in-law, having married the king's sister Eleanor in 1238. Simon was a younger son of a prominent French family. His father had been the military leader of the Albigensian Crusade, an effort to eradicate Cathars in southern France, a project in which Simon's brothers had also been involved. The Cathars were a Christian sect whose belief in two gods – one good, and one evil – was deemed heresy.

Simon bore the weight of this family expectation, seemingly seeking out a crusade of his own. He had expelled the Jewish population from his lands in Leicester when he took up the earldom, which he claimed via his paternal grandmother Amice de Beaumont, but Simon's crusade would turn out to be a political one. Henry and Simon were almost the same age, both around 50 years old, and their relationship was often rocky. Sometimes the best of friends, at other moments they almost came to blows.

Shocked by the king's terror, Simon asked Henry why he was still so afraid when the storm was already subsiding. The king replied, 'I fear thunder and lightning greatly, but by God's head, I fear you more than all the thunder and lightning in the world.' Offended, Simon expressed his loyalty to Henry, adding, 'it is your enemies, your destroyers, and false flatterers that you ought to fear.' Simon was prominent among the council established by the Provisions of Oxford, and Henry may have viewed his brother-in-law as the driving force behind it. The relationship between the two men was in decline once again.

In October 1258, the Provisions of Oxford were confirmed in proclamations issued in Latin, French and, for the first time, in English. The Provisions represented another moment as decisive as Magna Carta in 1215. Reform was no longer a bargain with the king but a weapon with which to threaten him. By the end of October, Parliament had heard about numerous breaches of the Provisions of Oxford, not by the king, but by the barons. Henry's oldest son, known as Lord Edward (and later King Edward I), was keen to listen and consider loosening the shackles that would one day be applied to him. The result was the creation of the Provisions of Westminster, which significantly watered down the Oxford version, just as the 1217 Magna Carta had made the 1215 Charter more palatable. In the aftermath of this further readjustment of the political relationships in England, Henry visited Paris to sign the treaty that ended his claims to the Angevin continental lands, except Gascony. There would be no more chasing lost shadows across the sea. England had problems enough of its own.

When Henry returned to England in April 1260, he discovered that his worst fears had been proven right, and far worse besides. Simon de Montfort had been stirring up reforming zeal among the barons in what would become the earl's version of his family's crusading tradition. The worst news was that Lord Edward had taken the side of his uncle, who was also his godfather. Henry

was heard to lament, 'Let not my son come before me, for if I see him, I shall not be able to refrain from kissing him.' Family was of critical importance to Henry, and this breach cut him deeply. It was at this point that Henry produced letters from his papal overlord instructing him to ignore the Provisions of Oxford. He wrote to Louis IX of France and Lord Edward to ask for their help in freeing him from the bonds the barons sought to place on him. Louis offered an army for seven years if required, and Edward returned to his father's side. A tense quiet fell on the kingdom for a while.

The king's behaviour in using the Pope to sidestep what he had agreed to was too close to his father's behaviour for comfort. As Henry offered financial inducements to men to pledge fealty to him and to support his cause, the barons began raising their own forces. The Second Barons' War was looming over the kingdom within half a century of the first. In the summer of 1263, Simon de Montfort led an army into the capital. Henry and Eleanor were staying at the Tower of London, and, when Eleanor tried to take a barge upriver to join her son Edward outside the city, she was pelted with mud and stone until the barge was forced to turn round. Edward, who shared his father's attachment to family, never forgave the city for their treatment of his mother. On 15 July 1263, peace was agreed between Henry and Simon, brokered by the king's brother Richard. Astonishingly for an English king, Henry agreed to allow Louis IX to mediate the disputes.

Henry agreed once again to be bound by the Provisions of Oxford and oversaw some reform to address perceived abuses in government that diffused baronial annoyance. Just as everything seemed to be calming down, Henry made a characteristic misjudgement. He demanded the handover of castles on the south coast, as well as control of the Cinque Ports.

Henry's grasping sparked fears that he was seeking to make way for an army from France to land on the south coast. The king travelled to Dover Castle to demand it was handed over but was unable to enforce his will.

As he headed back to London, Henry found that Simon and an army had camped at Southwark, blocking his way across the Thames and back into the city. A confrontation was avoided

CINQUE PORTS

This group of ports took its name from the French for the Five Harbours and comprised Hastings, New Romney, Hythe, Dover and Sandwich. The grouping emerged during the reign of Edward the Confessor and acquired concessions from the Crown in return for providing ships when required.

when Henry reconfirmed again his willingness to be bound by the Provisions of Oxford. In January 1264, Henry left for France to hear King Louis's verdict regarding the disputes in England. Simon was unable to travel as a result of being thrown from his horse and breaking his leg. Unsurprisingly, Louis found in Henry's favour, deploring the attack on Henry's sovereignty by his barons. The Provisions were to be scrapped and never relied on again.

Even before Henry returned to England, Simon's sons, Simon and Henry, were planning an uprising with Llywelyn ap Gruffudd in Wales. Richard ordered the smashing of all bridges over the River Severn with the exception of Gloucester and then waited. As soon as the king and his son returned, Lord Edward sped from the south coast to meet his uncle, Richard. The plan was clearly for Edward to impose royal authority on his father's behalf. From Gloucester Castle, Edward negotiated an agreement with the de Montfort brothers that offered the promise of further reform again. The brothers' withdrawal infuriated ap Gruffudd and the Earl of Derby, who had risked much to support them, and the alliance fell apart. However, Simon – the Senior, that is – continued to gather men at Kenilworth Castle in the Midlands.

When Henry returned to Dover Castle in an effort to secure the Cinque Ports again, Simon seized his opportunity and sped south, reaching Lewes for a showdown with the king's larger force. On 14 May 1264, the royal army was arrayed outside the town at the bottom of a slope. Henry controlled the centre, Richard the left wing and Edward the vanguard on the right. Still incapacitated by his broken leg, Simon was thought to be among the Londoners in his army on the left flank. When the fighting began, Edward charged furiously at the Londoners,

LISTEN TO THE
PODCAST

Henry III

as keen to punish them as he was to reach Simon. As he flung open Simon's carriage door, Edward was furious to discover he had been tricked. Simon was, in fact, on a horse on the right flank of his army, directing an attack from there. With Edward occupied chasing the Londoners from the battlefield, Simon focussed on Henry's force. The Battle of Lewes ended with Henry forced to surrender to Simon de Montfort. Richard and his son Henry of Almain (Henry of Germany) were captured after taking refuge in a windmill. Edward returned too late to save his father or the Crown – and was also taken captive.

Simon de Montfort's crusading zeal for reform in England had seen a Frenchman take the King of England hostage. As he began establishing his control over the realm, it remained to be seen whether he could fare any better than Henry. England had lost continental territory, tying the ruler to the island and focussing the attention of those who had lost land overseas on what remained and the institution they blamed for the loss. Simon believed he knew how to handle the matter better than the king. As he marched north from Lewes to London, King Henry III of England and his heir among his prisoners, he was confident he could deliver what he had demanded, and Henry had avoided, for so long.

Chapter 6

Rebuilding and Expanding England

Simon de Montfort's Parliament : The Battle of Evesham : The Statutes of Marlborough : Henry III's legacies : Edward I conquers Wales : The Scottish succession crisis : Codification of the law : Expulsion of Jews from England : William Wallace : Edward II's favourites : The Despenser Wars : Queen Isabella and Mortimer invade England : Execution of Hugh Despenser the Younger

An epic poem was written in the aftermath of the Battle of Lewes, known as the Song of Lewes. It offers an insight into the principles of its victor, Simon de Montfort. 'The king shall keep the natives in their rank, and by this management shall rejoice in ruling. But if he has sought to degrade his own men, has overturned their rank, it is in vain that he will ask, why when so deranged they do not obey him; nay, they would be mad if they were to do so.' It was the king's job to keep his people in line. But, the poet argued, if he failed the barons should do it for him.

Simon sought to base his government on the Provisions of Oxford, for which he had fought so hard. Though Henry would

SIMON DE MONTFORT'S PARLIAMENT

Simon summoned Parliament to open on 20 January 1265, and it would sit for two months. Elected representatives appeared, but this was not an innovation. It is not even certain that adding representatives from the towns to the country knights was new, either. The real novelties of Simon's Parliament lay in a session being summoned by someone other than the king for the first time and in seeking advice from Parliament to inform policy. The second of these is the more important point for the development of Parliament during the medieval period. It was the first time that Parliament was recorded as a forum to debate policy and inform decisions.

remain as king, the council would make all decisions in consultation with Parliament.

As he toured the kingdom, Simon sought to install the Provisions of Oxford and secure the south coast against invasion from France. This became more likely as the queen raised forces there to help her husband and son, who were in Simon's custody. As Simon negotiated an alliance with the Welsh leader Llywelyn ap Gruffudd to shore up support against the lords of the Welsh Marches, he based himself at Hereford and had Lord Edward brought there. On 28 May 1265, presumably a bright spring morning, Edward was permitted to ride outside the castle under guard. He appeared keen to make the most of his opportunity, as he rode each horse hard in turn. It was only when the prince got into the saddle of the last horse that his guards realised what was going on. Edward thanked them for providing him with the last fit horse, joked that they would not be able to chase on the other, exhausted horses, and waved them farewell. He rode hard to meet Roger Mortimer, a powerful Marcher baron, to begin unpicking what Simon had done.

Simon was finding it difficult to maintain the support he had initially enjoyed. One chronicler drew parallels with the language around the Anarchy (1138–1153), complaining that England 'trembled with the horrors of war' for more than a year. The restrictions placed on the king did not sit well with everyone. It did not help that Simon began giving key offices and grants of lands and incomes to his own sons. As a reformer of corruption who complained about favourites, he was becoming the monster he had campaigned to slay. The earl also sent word to the Continent that England was self-sufficient and required no foreign imports. Chroniclers were bemused as inflation gripped the realm. The price of items such as wine, wax, salt, iron, steel and cloth rocketed as they became suddenly scarce. After Edward's escape, Simon's problems increased exponentially.

Edward received word that Simon's namesake son, Simon the Younger, had set up camp at Kenilworth Castle, possibly to gather reinforcements. Speeding the 50 miles east, he caught his cousin unawares. Although Simon the Younger managed to get inside the castle, most of the barons and men-at-arms with him were captured along with Simon's banners. The elder Simon soon made for Worcester to hunt Edward, reaching Evesham on 3 August. The king and his captor lodged at the abbey there. When Edward himself drew near to Evesham, he unfurled the banner of Simon the Younger. Believing his son had arrived to reinforce him, Simon was utterly unprepared by the time he realised he had been tricked.

The Battle of Evesham

Lord Edward's army divided in two and blocked the paths out of Evesham, trapping Simon against the River Avon. When Edward rode onto the field, he wore a tabard over his armour displaying a red cross on a white background. His men wore the same, now familiar device. This was the first time an English army had taken to the field under the badge of St George. Simon's oldest son Henry pleaded with his father to escape, but the earl refused, reflecting his 'bloodline is known to be so illustrious as one who was never wont to flee from battle'. He would not ruin his family's reputation by running away.

LISTEN TO THE
PODCAST

Henry III vs Simon
de Montfort

When the Battle of Evesham began on 4 August 1265, it was a furious affair. Edward tasked a squad of a dozen of his finest knights with finding Simon and killing him. They were swift in their work.

William de Nangis, a chronicler, noted

that Simon 'defended himself like an impregnable tower', but he was hunted down and brutally killed. Not satisfied with simply slaying the earl, Edward's death squad began to dismember his body. William de Nangis continued that 'at the very summit of his noble deeds they rendered him headless, torn to pieces limb by limb and with parts of his manhood amputated'. Another source claims Simon's body did not bleed as he was hacked apart, and that he wore a hair shirt next to his skin. Simon's head was claimed by Roger Mortimer, who sent it home as a gift for his wife. Simon's oldest son, Henry, was among the dead and another son, Guy, was wounded and captured.

Somewhere in the melee was Henry, who had been put in armour and planted among Simon's men. As he was attacked, he cursed, 'By the love of God', and 'By God's head', shouting, 'I am Henry, the old king of England', pleading 'I am too old to fight'. The king was saved and brought to his son. On 7 August, three days after the battle, Henry issued proclamations announcing his full resumption of authority. It was not until the New Year that Simon the Younger surrendered at Kenilworth. He was given a pension by his uncle the king in recognition of his good treatment and early release of Henry's brother Richard and his son Henry of Almain, but was required to leave England for a time. Simon and his brother Guy would later find and murder Henry of Almain in a church in Viterbo, Italy, and Simon died later the same year in what was seen as God's punishment for the deed.

Rebuilding the English Monarchy

Edward began to lead the reforming of his father's government. He had a vested interest in rebuilding the royal authority that would one day be his. The prince was given responsibility for the protection of English merchants and for granting licences to foreign merchants to return to England, and placed in control of the Cinque Ports. Although Simon the Younger had surrendered, some still held out at Kenilworth against Henry and Edward. When those known as the 'disinherited' were forced to give up Kenilworth, some seized the Isle of Ely to continue their resistance. Eventually, the breach was sealed after an agreement was negotiated by Richard.

At the end of 1267, Henry issued the Statutes of Marlborough. The 29 articles enshrined the Provisions of Westminster, the watered-down version of the Provisions of Oxford, which had included various legal and administrative demands made by barons. The Statutes remained in force for centuries to follow. Four remain on the statute books of the United Kingdom today. Henry and Edward would work in partnership for the remainder of Henry's rule in a way that Henry II must have hoped for when he made his son Junior King. Together they set about rebuilding the royal authority that had stuttered throughout Henry's rule before it was shattered by Simon's rebellion. Henry also indulged his passion for building. His devotion to Edward the Confessor as his favourite saint led him to rebuild the Confessor's church at Westminster. The abbey that was consecrated on 13 October 1269 is the basis of the Westminster Abbey that remains today, and the Cosmati Pavement before the high altar was installed at the king's commission. Henry had the body of Edward the Confessor translated to its current position at the centre of the Shrine of St Edward the Confessor and earmarked the place the saint-king had rested for more than two centuries for his own grave when the time came.

When a fresh crusade to the Holy Land was preached, Edward took up the call. He left England on 19 August 1270. In February of the following year, Henry wrote to his son to tell him he was ill beyond hope of recovery, though he did rally. In the months that followed, however, the king's nephew Henry of Almain was murdered by his cousins on his way home from the crusade. The king's brother Richard, a stalwart of his rule, died on 2 April 1272. Henry may well have been left feeling rather isolated. By May, Henry was asking Philip III of France to be excused from his journey to pay homage for lands in Gascony due to declining health. On 16 November 1272, aged 65 and after 56 years as king, Henry died. A few days later, he was buried in the space previously occupied by Edward the Confessor.

One of Henry's innovations altered the nature of kingship in England for ever. The period of interregnum had been endlessly troublesome. Henry amended the law so that, from his death onwards, a new king succeeded at the moment of the old king's death. The notion of 'The King is dead, long live the King' was born. In 1272, it meant that England had a new king, Edward I, despite the fact that he was several thousand miles away in the Holy Land. Edward had proven himself an excellent general and soldier. Now, he would have to prove himself a good king, a judgement that eluded his father. Yet before he even left the Holy Land, Edward first had to survive an assassination attempt in which he killed his attacker but sustained a wound from a poisoned dagger that delayed his departure. Only after almost two years since Henry's death was Edward crowned, on 19 August 1274 and aged 35. The bolstered structures of medieval England had survived their first test.

The Conquest of Wales

In Wales, Llywelyn found himself in a tricky situation when his brother Dafydd and another Welsh prince, Gruffydd ap Gwenwynwyn, tried to assassinate him and then fled to Edward. Ongoing trouble along the Welsh Marches added to Llywelyn's problems so that he failed to do homage to Edward as required by the terms of the 1267 Treaty of Montgomery. Llywelyn further antagonised Edward by arranging to marry Eleanor de Montfort, Simon's daughter. In late 1276, Edward attacked Llywelyn. A large part of the king's army was made up of Welshmen, demonstrating the lack of support Llywelyn enjoyed among his own countrymen. Llywelyn was forced to surrender and agree to the Treaty of Aberconwy in November 1277, which reduced the land he ruled to Gwynedd in northwest Wales, though he was permitted to retain the title Prince of Wales.

The unsteady peace lasted until 1282 when Dafydd moved into open revolt against Edward. Despite their previous issues, Llywelyn felt compelled to support his brother. Edward now abandoned the idea of simply trying to bring Llywelyn into line

RING OF IRON

In the aftermath of his conquest, Edward built a series of castles to encircle North Wales and enforce his control. Many were built under the supervision of master architect James of Saint George, whom Edward had met in Savoy on his way back from the crusade. Mighty castles at Flint, Hawarden, Rhuddlan, Builth, Aberystwyth, Denbigh, Caernarfon, Conwy, Harlech and Beaumaris wrote Edward's victory into stone.

and set about conquering Wales. Welsh guerrilla tactics initially brought success, but Llywelyn was lured into a trap and killed at the Battle of Orewin Bridge on 11 December 1282. Dafydd was captured in the summer of 1283 and executed, his head displayed on London Bridge. In 1284 Edward published the Statute of Rhuddlan, which formally absorbed Wales into England and installed English law and governmental systems to replace Welsh ones. The same year, Edward's son, another Edward, was born

EDWARD I
IN WALES

0   20   40

ANGLESEY

CARNARVON

LINCOLN

FLINT

COUNTY PALATINE
OF CHESTER

MERIONETH

FITZALAN

CORBET

MORTIMER

KINGDOM
OF ENGLAND

CARDIGAN

CARMARTHEN

MARSHALL

LANCASTER

BOHUN

CLARE

PRINCIPALITY OF NORTH WALES
CREATED BY EDWARD I

MARCHER LORDSHIPS

PRINCIPALITY OF GWYNEDD

at Caernarfon Castle. In 1301, the boy would become the first English heir to be invested as Prince of Wales.

Rebellions continued in Wales, a serious one arising in 1294 under the leadership of Madog ap Llywelyn, a relative of Llywelyn ap Gruffudd, who would become known as Llywelyn the Last.

Much of Edward's focus was on securing peace in Europe that would facilitate another crusade in which he hoped to take part. Despite his efforts, the plans came to nothing, hampered by ongoing tensions between France and Aragon and then by the fall of Acre, the last Christian foothold in the Holy Land. On 28 November 1290, personal tragedy struck for Edward too. His wife of 36 years, Eleanor of Castile, died. The couple were devoted to each other, and her passing seemed to harden Edward. Eleanor died in Nottinghamshire and Edward had her body transported back to London for burial. At every place the funeral cortège stopped, he ordered the construction of a stone memorial. Eleanor Crosses stood at Lincoln, Grantham, Stamford, Geddington, Hardingstone, Stony Stratford, Woburn, Dunstable, St Albans, Waltham, Westcheap and Charing (which became known as Charing Cross for the Eleanor Cross there). Only those at Geddington, Hardingstone and Waltham still survive as monuments to a king's love for his queen.

The Scottish Succession Crisis

The cordial relationship with Scotland fostered by Henry III endured into Edward's reign. Alexander III was Edward's brother-in-law. But when Alexander died on 19 March 1286, it sparked a crisis that would engulf Scotland and dominate the rest of Edward's reign. Alexander's only living heir was his three-year-old granddaughter, Margaret, known as the Maid of Norway. (Alexander's daughter, also named Margaret, had married Eric II,

King of Norway.) Until she came to Scotland, six men were appointed Guardians of the Realm to rule in Margaret's name. Edward negotiated the Treaty of Birgham with the Guardians, arranging for his six-year-old son Edward of Caernarfon to marry Margaret but allowing Scotland to remain independent of English overlordship. In 1290, aged seven, Margaret finally sailed from Norway to make the match but fell ill on the voyage and died in Orkney. With her loss, Scotland was left with no obvious heir and fell into a succession dispute.

Various nobles prepared to press their claims to the throne. The Bishop of St Andrews wrote to Edward to inform him of Margaret's death and ask for his help in promoting the claim of John Balliol, Lord of Galloway. Another lord, Robert Bruce, also appealed for support from Edward in a document known as the Appeal of the Seven Earls. As the threat of civil war grew, the Guardians invited Edward to judge the claims and select the next king in what became known as the Great Cause. They felt the friendly relationship they enjoyed made the king an interested ally. However unwittingly, the Guardians reignited the question of English overlordship of Scotland. Edward moved north with an army and demanded the Scots delegates meet him at Norham Castle on the English side of the border. Edward demanded that the Guardians and all the candidates recognise him as their overlord before he would deliver his decision. In return, the Guardians insisted that only a King of Scotland could make that decision.

Edward sent instructions throughout England to seek out documentary evidence to support English overlordship of Scotland as he proceeded. Thirteen men presented their claim to the Scots throne to Edward. Only two, John Balliol and Robert Bruce, were serious competitors. Edward demanded that both men swore to recognise him as overlord if chosen. With little option, they agreed. In an instant, Edward had, technically at least, taken possession of Scotland. He was no longer a neutral mediator, but the judge of claims to the Scottish throne.

In November 1292, after more than a year of debate, Edward presented his decision. He concluded that John Balliol's claim was stronger based on primogeniture. His line of descent was deemed senior to that of Robert Bruce. Balliol became King of Scots, but his agreement to hold his throne as Edward's vassal led to him being given the nickname Toom Tabard, Scots for 'empty coat', mocking his inability to be an effective, independent king. John's rule became increasingly unpopular as Edward demanded homage, constant demonstrations of his power over Scotland, and money to fund his military designs on France. In 1294, Philip IV of France seized Gascony from Edward and war between England and France moved closer. In July 1295, the Scottish nobility established a new council to take over the government, effectively re-establishing the Guardians of the Realm. The council of 12 sought a treaty of mutual aid between Scotland and France in the first agreement that would form the Auld Alliance, a partnership formed in opposition to England that would be central to the events of the following centuries.

Furious at the new alliance, Edward launched an invasion of Scotland that ignited what became the Wars of Scottish Independence. Edward took Dunbar Castle in April 1296 and, on 10 July at Stracathro near Melrose, John Balliol abdicated his hard-won position as King of Scots. He was imprisoned in the Tower of London until he was eventually allowed to leave for his family's lands in France. When his baggage was inspected, it was discovered that John was trying to take the Scots crown, royal seal, and a large quantity of gold and silver with him. Edward allowed him to keep the

LISTEN TO THE
PODCAST

The Origins of
Scottish
Independence

valuables, sent the crown to the Shrine of St Thomas Becket at Canterbury, and kept the seal for himself. Seals were used as a form of signature to give authority to documents, and the royal seal was the method by which a king gave his instructions and passed laws.

Edward's control of the seal tightened his grip on Scotland. He installed Englishmen to govern Scotland, and also took the Stone of Destiny, also known as the Stone of Scone.

THE STONE OF SCONE

Kings of Scots were traditionally crowned sitting on the Stone of Scone. Edward ordered the creation of a new coronation chair for England with space beneath it for the Stone of Scone. Every monarch of England and the United Kingdom since has been crowned on that throne with the Stone of Scone beneath them. The Stone was returned to Scotland in 1996 and is kept at Edinburgh Castle with the Scottish crown jewels. In 2023, it was sent to London to be placed into the coronation chair for the crowning of King Charles III.

Codifying Edward's Rule

Alongside his efforts to extend his authority into Wales and Scotland, Edward took a great interest in the law. In part, it offered a mechanism to rebuild the royal authority that had been damaged during his father's reign, but it also helped the king understand his rights and made laws universal across England. The creation of documents such as the Provisions of Oxford in Henry's reign held appeal to Edward. Robert Burnell was appointed Chancellor in 1274 and held the office until 1292. As early as 1275, he issued the Statute of Westminster, which codified the law into 51 chapters. Chapter Five, which requires free elections, remains on the United Kingdom statute books to this day. This was followed up by the Statute of Westminster in 1275 (sometimes referred to as the Statute of Westminster II), which sought to reform and codify the law further, including land law and local policing. The codification of England's law added to institutions like the Exchequer to make English government robust and centralised and has earned Edward the nickname, 'the English Justinian', an allusion to the Byzantine Emperor Justinian I, who sought to rebuild the Roman Empire in the 6th century.

Edward was also responsible for the targeting of the Jewish population in England. Jews became associated with money-lending because Christians were forbidden from charging interest on loans, a practice known as usury. In 1275, Edward issued the Statute of Jewry to outlaw loans with interest. In 1279, the king set out to tackle coin clipping. This was a crime that saw people clip a small amount off a coin before spending it. The coin in circulation was devalued, which was considered to impact negatively on the Crown's reputation, and the clippings would accumulate to become of value themselves, perhaps in forging coins. As part of Edward's crackdown, he rounded up the heads of Jewish households and executed around 300 of them. Matters came to a head in 1290 with the Edict of Expulsion. Edward ordered all Jews to leave England, seizing their goods, money and debts. It would remain illegal to be a Jew in England until the 1650s, when it was finally reversed by Oliver Cromwell's government of the Commonwealth.

First War of Scottish Independence

As taxation and constant calls to military service caused friction, Edward was presented with a document known as The Remonstrances. Submitted by the earls of Norfolk and Hereford, it aimed to encapsulate the feeling across the kingdom that Edward was taxing the realm into poverty and requiring unreasonable levels of military service. Yet Edward was ultimately saved from having to confront these problems by a renewal of trouble in Scotland that galvanised the kingdom. After Edward's enforced settlement of 1296, opposition had grown quickly in Scotland. It was led by Andrew de Moray, who was joined by William Wallace. Moray and Wallace attacked an English army as it crossed the River Forth at Stirling. By waiting until the army was separated on either side, the Scots forces were able to deal a crushing blow at the Battle of Stirling Bridge on 11 September 1297.

Edward united his unsettled barons against the threat, and defeated Wallace at the Battle of Falkirk on 22 July 1298. The Scots appealed to Pope Boniface VIII to become their overlord, as John had done in 1215. Although the Pope was keen on the idea, Edward ensured that it made no progress. Wallace was betrayed to the English in 1305 and taken to London for a public, and gruesome, execution.

Over the following years, Edward regained control of Scotland, aided by Robert the Bruce, the grandson of the claimant to the throne during the Great Cause. Matters changed again in February 1306 when Bruce murdered his rival John Comyn and had himself crowned King of Scotland on 25 March. His campaign to restore Scottish independence faltered when he was routed by an English army at the Battle of Methven in June 1306. Following this defeat, he went into hiding for a period, an episode that would later give rise to the story that his observation of a spider creating its web convinced him not to give up.

Robert re-emerged in 1307 to win a victory at the Battle of Loudoun Hill on 10 May. This development caused Edward to move north himself despite his failing health. The journey saw the king contract dysentery, and, at Burgh by Sands in Cumbria, on 7 July 1307, Edward died at the age of 68. His body was returned to London for burial at Westminster Abbey. In the 16th century, an inscription was added to the tomb that translates from Latin as 'Here is Edward I, Hammer of the Scots, 1308. Keep the Troth.' The epithet Hammer of the Scots has been applied to Edward

since then, though in many ways he left his plan to subjugate Scotland only partly complete. His son, Edward of Caernarfon, would be required to take on the project as King Edward II.

Edward II's Favourites

The coronation of Edward II took place on 25 February 1308 alongside that of his wife, Isabella of France, the only daughter of Philip IV of France. Edward was his parents' fourth son. He was 26 when he became king. He was widely described as handsome, athletic and strikingly large, and it may have appeared that he would relish taking on his father's incomplete military work. However, Edward II's first act was to send word to his closest friend Piers Gaveston to return to England. Edward's partiality for Gaveston had led his father to banish the man, and in one furious exchange the younger Edward had tried to convince his father to make Gaveston Count of Ponthieu in Gascony. Edward I had sworn at his son, shouting, 'Now you want to give lands away – you who never gained any? As the Lord lives, were it not for fear of breaking up the kingdom, you should never enjoy your inheritance!' The recurring obsession with favourites, those who dominated the king's ear and drove policy, was to prove an irresolvable problem for Edward.

Edward and Isabella were married in France on 25 January 1308. During the celebrations, a group of English barons presented Edward with the Boulogne Agreement. The document set out how loyalty to the Crown of England could be separated from loyalty to the present king. It is unclear whether this was a backlash against the worst extremes of Edward I's rule, or due to concern caused by the character of Edward II. In April, the Agreement was produced in Parliament as a Declaration, but its true intent remains something of a mystery. It may have sought to extend protection for those criticising the monarch by protecting them from accusations of treason. The return of Piers Gaveston may well have driven the barons' actions, as in May 1308 he was driven into a second period of exile. A year later, he returned. When Parliament was summoned in 1309 and in 1310, many lords refused to attend.

In March 1310, Edward was presented with a set of ordinances for the reform of his government. The Lords Ordainers, as the group were known, included the earls of Pembroke, Lincoln, Lancaster, Hereford, Warwick, Arundel, Richmond and Gloucester, as well as the Archbishop of Canterbury, six bishops, and other barons. The Lords Ordainers warned the king 'they would not have him for king, nor keep the fealty that they had sworn to him' unless he agreed to the reforms. Deposition had not been attempted before but was now being used to threaten the king. The dangers of Edward's attachment became clearer when he offered to accept 40 of the articles if one was dropped: the requirement to exile Gaveston again. Edward was forced to agree, but, once again, the banishment did not last long.

On 13 January 1312, Gaveston met Edward at Knaresborough, and five days later the king formally revoked his exile. Gaveston was soon trapped within Scarborough Castle and taken into custody by the Earl of Pembroke. In the early morning of 10 June, the Earl of Warwick found where Gaveston was being held and had him moved to Warwick Castle. On 19 June, Piers was moved to Kenilworth Castle, which belonged to Edward's cousin the Earl of Lancaster. From there, he was taken to Blacklow Hill nearby, and the earls of Lancaster, Hereford and Arundel looked on as the king's favourite was executed by beheading. Edward never forgave those responsible for Gaveston's death, leading to a decade of problems, particularly with his cousin Thomas, Earl of Lancaster.

Isabella gave birth to the couple's first child at Windsor Castle on 13 November 1312. He was also named Edward. There has been speculation for centuries about the nature of Edward's relationship with his favourites. Whether he engaged in sexual relationships with them is uncertain, but he was clearly close to his wife. During a visit to France in 1313, the couple's tent caught fire as they slept and Edward emerged naked and carried Isabella to safety. In 1317, the king gave the county of Cornwall, which had belonged to Gaveston, to his wife. In early 1318, when his stepmother passed away, Edward ensured Isabella received the dower queen's lands and incomes, and a month later he gave her the county of Ponthieu in Gascony, which he had once incurred the wrath of his father for attempting to gift to Gaveston.tried to give to Gaveston, incurring his father's wrath.

Edward I's plans in Scotland received little or no attention from Edward II. He did invade Scotland in 1313 when Robert the Bruce laid siege to Stirling Castle, which was held by an English force. On 23–24 June 1314, Robert the Bruce won a decisive victory at the Battle of Bannockburn, a critical moment in the War of Scottish Independence. Over two days of sporadic

GREAT OFFICES OF STATE

Chamberlain was one of the nine Great Offices of State and was responsible for managing the royal household. The Great Offices had an order of authority. The highest office was the Lord High Steward of England. This was followed by the Lord High Chancellor, then the Lord High Treasurer. Next came the Lord President of the Council, the Lord Keeper of the Privy Seal, then the Lord Great Chamberlain. The remaining offices were the Lord High Constable, the Earl Marshal, and then the Lord High Admiral.

fighting, English cavalry was hampered by small ditches and ultimately defeated.

By the end of the decade, Edward had fallen under the spell of a new favourite. Hugh Despenser the Younger, a name used to differentiate him from his father, Hugh Despenser the Elder, became Edward's chamberlain in 1318.

Several favourites had come and gone since Gaveston, though he was probably Edward's favourite among them. Although the barons had often objected to the power these men wielded, Hugh Despenser the Younger was beyond the pale. He accumulated power for his own aggrandisement and made no effort to hide his corruption. Queen Isabella objected to Despenser in a way she had not to other favourites. Despenser laid claim to lands in Wales on the Gower Peninsula. Others with interests there rebelled, including several Marcher Lords. Prominent among them was Roger Mortimer of Wigmore, a powerful Marcher baron. The group demanded Despenser's exile, threatening to depose Edward if he did not agree. The Despenser Wars erupted in May 1321. In August, Edward agreed to exile the father and son in the face of the Marcher Lords' early military successes. By December, Edward had changed his mind once again, and ordered the arrest of the rebels in the Marches.

The Despenser Wars

Many tried to flee to the lands of the Earl of Lancaster to seek his support. Their way was blocked by the Sheriff of Cumberland, who engaged the Earl and the other rebels at the Battle of Boroughbridge on 16 March 1322. The sheriff won and was created Earl of Carlisle for his service. Lancaster was captured and taken before his cousin the king while dressed in the tunic of a servant to humiliate him. Lancaster was tried for treason and

GRUESOME ENDS

To be hung, drawn and quartered became the standard punishment for treason. The drawing part came first and referred to being dragged behind a horse to the place of execution. Over time, it became more common to place the condemned on a wooden hurdle to prevent them from banging their head too much and escaping the rest of their punishment as many were knocked unconscious or even killed. The victim would then be hanged, ensuring that their neck did not break. Once they had been strangled almost unconscious, they would be cut down and their belly sliced open. Their stomach would be thrown into a fire beside them so that with their last breaths they would smell their own insides burning. Once dead, the body would be beheaded and then cut into quarters to be distributed around the kingdom. The head was often displayed on London Bridge. The cruelty and display of body parts were meant to provide a deterrent to those considering acts of treason.

condemned to be hung, drawn and quartered.

In 1324, relations with France hit a crisis again. The third of Queen Isabella's brothers to follow their father was Charles IV after the deaths of Louis X and Philip V. The new reign required Edward to travel to France to pay homage to Charles, something an English king was never keen to do, and certainly not three times in quick succession. When Edward delayed, Charles seized Gascony. For some reason, Edward chose this moment to take back the estates he had given his wife in Cornwall. He may have planned to make Hugh Despenser the Younger the new Earl of Cornwall. In March 1325, Isabella travelled to France to seek peace between her brother and her husband. It was agreed that Edward should give homage for Gascony by 29 August 1325, or lose it for ever. After much toing and froing, Edward sent his 12-year-old son Edward of Windsor in his place.

Isabella now made her move. She had an intense dislike for Hugh Despenser that she had not exhibited toward Edward's other favourites. Whether he was one too many, or, as the reactions of others to Hugh suggest, deemed detestable and dangerous, she refused to return home or send their son back to England until Despenser was dealt with permanently. To add to the pressure, Isabella arranged a marriage for their son, a serious diplomatic matter that ought to have fallen to Edward and the nobility to decide. Isabella was joined in exile by a number of the rebels who had escaped punishment after the Despenser Wars. Chief among them was Roger Mortimer, who had escaped from the Tower of London in 1323 and fled abroad. Stories would emerge that Mortimer and the queen became lovers at some point, though there is no evidence to support such a claim. What is clear is that the two shared a political goal: the removal of Hugh Despenser.

On 24 September 1326, Isabella, Mortimer, several other lords and around 1,000 men landed at Orwell in Suffolk. Several bishops and nobles, including the new Earl of Lancaster, brother

of the executed Thomas, joined the rebels. Edward placed a bounty of £1,000 on Mortimer's head. Isabella placed a bounty of £2,000 on Despenser's. Edward fled into Wales and made for the coast. Isabella issued a memorandum that criticised her husband for 'going away from his realm with Hugh le Despenser'. Edward of Windsor was appointed Guardian of the Realm as though the king was absent. Isabella laid siege to Hugh the Elder's castle at Bristol and won it swiftly. The 56-year-old was hauled to the market square in his armour and hanged in front of a crowd. Once dead, his corpse was beheaded. The body was fed to dogs, and the head paraded to Winchester on the end of a spear. Things were getting dangerously out of hand.

Edward II was apprehended on 16 November 1326 near Llantrisant in Wales. He had no more than a handful of his household left with him. Hugh the Younger was among them. He was taken before Isabella, who ordered him moved to London for a public trial and execution. Hugh went on hunger strike and the decision was taken to try him at Hereford instead. His conviction a foregone conclusion, Hugh was forced to ride through the city on 24 November 1326 with his coat of arms reversed, the mark of a disgraced knight. A crown of nettles was jammed onto his head. In the centre of Hereford, a 50-foot-high scaffold was erected to ensure everyone had a good view of the horrors to follow. Hugh was drawn to the scaffold, hanged, and then cut open. As his guts sizzled in a brazier beside him, he was castrated too, his manhood also thrown into the flames. Only then was he beheaded. His head was sent to be displayed on London Bridge, the four quarters of his body to Carlisle, York, Bristol and Dover. It would be four years before the parts of his body were reunited and buried at Tewkesbury Abbey.

All that remained was to try to deal with Edward II.

Chapter 7

The Hundred Years' War Begins

Edward II is deposed : The murder of Edward II? :
Edward III assumes authority : The Second War of Scottish
Independence : War with France begins : The Battle of Crecy :
The Black Death : The Battle of Poitiers :
Richard II becomes king as a boy

The aim of Queen Isabella had been to rid herself of Hugh Despenser the Younger, the royal chamberlain of her husband Edward II who, through his acquisition of land and titles, found himself despised by England's nobility. That goal was gruesomely realised at Hereford in November 1326. His execution meant Isabella's immediate problems were over, though she might have worried about who would come next and whether they might be worse than Despenser. A greater problem was the barons who had supported Isabella, particularly Roger Mortimer. The king's wife, son and two half-brothers who had joined the revolt might find forgiveness. Others would not. A vengeful Edward would seek to punish them for the loss of another favourite. Freeing Edward would be a death sentence for Mortimer and his peers.

A council meeting discussed the problems and decided that Edward should abdicate in favour of his son and then be allowed to live out his life in peace. But the question on everyone's lips was how this could be achieved. No king had been deposed like this in England's history. How could an anointed monarch, chosen by God, be made back into an ordinary man? Could it ever be legally or spiritually binding? With necessity as the midwife to invention, Mortimer and his allies decided to have the abdication put through Parliament. This underlined the institution's role as England's premier vehicle for legal authority and legitimacy. It also saw Parliament move closer to the role the Anglo-Saxon Witan had enjoyed in choosing who should be king. That power was being extended now to the right to remove a king deemed too bad to be allowed to continue. Edward II's fate was the conclusion of questions that had remained open for more than a century since the reign of his great-grandfather, John.

Even as Parliament assembled in January 1327, nobody knew whether what they did was legal, nor what would happen if Edward refused to play his part. When Edward was informed that he was no longer King of England, he reflected, 'I greatly lament that I have so utterly failed my people, but I could not be other than I am.' Edward was famed for indulging in hobbies that bemused his kingdom. Ditching, thatching and swimming were not deemed suitable pursuits for a king. He preferred the company of labourers to that of lords, and his repeated attachment to favourites had proven unbearable. On 25 January 1327, Edward of Windsor became King Edward III at the age of 14. His coronation took place at Westminster Abbey, on the coronation chair his grandfather had created, on 2 February. Edward II was referred to from this point onwards as Sir Edward of Caernarfon and was placed into the custody of his cousin Henry, Earl of Lancaster.

The final fate of Edward II is less than certain. His custody was transferred to Thomas, Lord Berkeley, Mortimer's son-in-law and

LISTEN TO THE
PODCAST

The Death of
Edward II

a rebel imprisoned in 1322, and Sir John Maltravers. Edward was held at Berkeley Castle. When Robert the Bruce invaded England in 1327, there was an attempt to free the former king while Mortimer was distracted in the north. During the same year, 26 people were arrested at Caernarfon Castle, Edward's birthplace, for a plot to rescue him. Edward's date of death is given as 21 September 1327. He reportedly died at Berkeley Castle, perhaps murdered, though the story that he was killed by the insertion of a red-hot poker into his rectum is a later invention. However, in 1330 Edward's half-brother was executed for trying to free him. In 1330, Lord Berkeley claimed he had never been aware that Sir Edward was dead. When Edward II truly died is uncertain. His tomb in Gloucester Cathedral may, or may not, contain his mortal remains.

Roger Mortimer and Queen Isabella ruled England as regents for the young Edward III after his coronation. Mortimer had himself made Earl of March to reinforce his dominance in the Welsh Marches. Rumours that he and the queen were lovers continued but remain unproven. Mortimer's rule became

THE FIESCHI LETTER

A document known as the Fieschi Letter, sent by an Italian priest to Edward III, claimed later that decade that Edward II had not died at all. Rather he was alive and well, having escaped Berkeley Castle, and was living in Italy. Additionally, in 1338 Edward III reportedly entertained and gave money to a man named William le Galeys – William the Welshman – who openly claimed to be his father.

increasingly high-handed as he revelled in his position of control over the teenage king. Eventually, Edward had had enough. On 19 October 1330, aged 17, Edward and a group of his friends snuck into Nottingham Castle using tunnels beneath it and burst into Mortimer's chamber. The earl was seized and, on 29 November, he was hanged like a common criminal at Tyburn in London.

The Second War of Scottish Independence

One of Edward III's first actions was to reignite war with Scotland. The Second War of Scottish Independence began in 1332 with an English-backed invasion of Scotland. Robert the Bruce died in 1329, leaving his six-year-old son David II in the care of a regent, the Earl of Moray. Edward Balliol, the son of John Balliol who had been forced to abdicate after Edward I's interventions, sought help from the English to press his own claim. Edward quietly backed an incursion into Scotland, and Balliol won a crushing victory at the Battle of Dupplin Moor southwest of Perth on 11 August against a force ten times the size of his own. On 24 September, Edward Balliol was crowned King of Scots at Scone. He gave Edward III estates in Scotland and the tactically crucial border town of Berwick, but within a few months Edward had been defeated at the Battle of Annan on 16 December by forces loyal to David II. Driven to England, Edward Balliol again sought English support.

Abandoning any secrecy, Edward III openly recognised Edward as King of Scots and provided him with military aid. On 19 July 1333, the English force won the Battle of Halidon Hill and Edward Balliol was reinstated to the Scots throne. Balliol would be deposed again in 1334, restored in 1335, and finally removed in 1336 in favour of David II. The Second War of Scottish

Independence lasted until 1357, and France would be dragged into the conflict as part of a wider European dispute. The early exchanges provided some military lessons for Edward III, which he was quick to learn, harness and deploy to devastating effect.

At the Battle of Dupplin Moor, the smaller force was victorious partly due to a novel battlefield tactic. The vast majority of the army fought on foot, having learned the lessons of Bannockburn. The novelty lay in dividing the archers and posting them on either side of the army's main body, the centre. Previously, archers would offer a volley of arrows from the front and then retreat behind the men-at-arms. The new tactic worked so well against greater numbers at Dupplin Moor that Edward repeated it at Halidon Hill. It would become a core element of the conflict that came to dominate Edward's reign: not with Scotland, but with France.

Edward III remained married to the woman his mother had chosen, Philippa of Hainault, until her death in 1369. The couple had a large brood of children: five sons and four daughters who

survived infancy. Edward had a strong interest in Arthurian legend, which he shared with his grandfather, Edward I. Two things preoccupied England during his years on the throne. One was man-made, the other a natural disaster. The first began in 1337 when Edward was 24. Unsurprisingly, the catalyst was homage to the French king for Gascony.

War with France

Philip VI had reigned as King of France since 1328. When Charles IV, the last of Edward's mother's brothers, died without an heir it created a crisis. There were two options for succession. One was Philip, then Count of Valois. He was a grandson of Philip III. The other candidate was a grandson of Philip IV, so was more closely connected to the throne. The problem was that he was also Edward III. The French had no desire for a foreign king and certainly not one who was already King of England. The French polity scrambled to find a solution and relied on Salic law, an ancient law code almost a thousand years old. They claimed that Salic law prevented the transmission of a claim through a female line, which was not true. However, it served the present need, and Edward III was overlooked because his claim was derived from his mother, Isabella.

As a result, Philip VI became the first king of the House of Valois. When he fell into dispute with Edward over homage for Gascony, Philip seized the region. In response, Edward reopened the debate of almost a decade earlier and laid claim not to Gascony but to Philip's Crown. As hostilities broke out, France had a much larger population and was wealthier. As France amassed a navy on its north coast, skirmishes broke out at sea near Cadzand and Arnemuiden. The first large battle of what would become known as the Hundred Years' War was a naval

THE CHEVAUCHÉE

The English employed lightning strikes with cavalry across the countryside. Known as the chevauchée, these raids sought to destroy crops and burn homes to drive home the idea that the lord of the region, or in this case the King of France, was incapable of protecting his subjects, and to suggest that the King of England could.

encounter on 24 June 1340. The Battle of Sluys raged all day and into the night. Hand-to-hand fighting was supplemented by archers and crossbowmen. The French tactic of chaining their fleet together backfired when the English won one ship and were able to move across the other French vessels with ease. Twenty French ships were sunk and more than 150 captured, with thousands of Frenchmen lost at sea.

The Battle of Crecy

Throughout the 1340s there were a series of land battles as Edward took the fight to Philip on French soil. The first major engagement came on 26 August 1346 at the Battle of Crecy. Using the tactics he had deployed in Scotland, Edward ordered all his men to dismount. They dug pits, each a foot wide and a foot deep, to hinder French cavalry, as the Scots had done to the English at Bannockburn. When the infantry lined up, archers were placed among them as they had been at Dupplin Moor and Halidon Hill. These were novel tactics on the Continent that the French had not encountered before.

The other innovation Edward tried at Crecy was the deployment of cannons on the battlefield. A relatively new introduction to Europe, they were being used in castle sieges, but Edward thought they might prove useful in the field, even if only to frighten the French horses. At a time when the loudest noise most people heard was the parish church bell, cannons were potentially terrifying. His plans laid, Edward took up a position in a nearby windmill that offered a good view of the site. As the French approached, they strained to get at the English. Philip realised he was losing control of his forces and ordered his crossbowmen to begin the attack before the king had even reached the battlefield. The Genoese crossbowmen approached, but most of their ammunition and protection were still in the rear with the baggage train. As the English longbows began to shoot, the chronicler Froissart recorded that they fell so thickly and evenly that they were like deadly snow.

As the shocked crossbowmen fell back, they encountered the enraged French cavalry in full charge. Many were trampled by their own allies. As barbed arrows bit the flesh of the horses, knights lost control of their mounts. As the main body of the

French army reached the field, they were greeted by an embarrassing scene of carnage and launched another attack. The English position and their pits funnelled the French to the English right, slowing their momentum and creating a bottleneck. Edward III had placed his 16-year-old son Edward, the Black Prince, Prince of Wales, at this hotspot. One eyewitness recorded that 'the young prince displayed marvellous courage standing in the front line against the enemy, running through horses, felling knights, crushing helmets under his blows, and all the while he encouraged his men pulling fallen friends to their feet and setting everyone an example.'

As the French pressed on, men reached Edward III to request help for his son. The king refused, replying, 'Go back to him and those who sent you and tell them from me that they are not to send for help again, whatever happens. As long as my son is still alive, tell them that my orders are that they should let the boy win his spurs for I wish the day to be his if God wills it, and that he and his companions shall have the honour of it.' When the prince was knocked to the ground, and his standard fell, his father relented and sent help, but by the time it arrived the prince was on his feet and fighting again fiercely. Against a vastly superior force, the English won at Crecy with their novel tactics.

Philip VI was injured by an arrow in the face after two horses were killed under him. Among the dead was John, the blind King of Bohemia. Determined not to miss the opportunity for glory, he had ordered two of his knights to lash their horses to his to lead him in between them. The three men were found dead, still together. Prince Edward was so struck by John's bravery that he adopted John's ostrich feather badge and motto, 'Ich Dein' – 'I serve'. The badge and motto are still used by the heir to the throne of the United Kingdom today. A week after the battle, Edward III's forces laid siege to Calais, a fortified seaport on

THE ORDER OF THE GARTER

With 26 members, the Order represents two tournament teams, one captained by the king, the other by the heir to the throne, each with 12 knights on their side, a structure that has endured ever since. Orders of chivalry usually had a badge or symbol to denote membership. Edward selected a garter for reasons that are also uncertain. One story relates that the Countess of Salisbury's garter slipped while she was dancing and inspired the king. Another claims that Richard I tied garters round the legs of his knights on crusade, and that Edward took his inspiration from their success. The garter may also have represented straps that held armour in place.

France's northern coast that would become a key part of England's story for two centuries. After almost a year, Calais surrendered on 3 August 1347.

In order to celebrate his achievements and galvanise the spirit of brotherhood created among the nobility, Edward established a new order of chivalry in 1348. There is some evidence that it was constituted in 1344, and other dates have been suggested so that the precise moment of its foundation remains unclear. The Order of the Garter is among the most famous orders in the world and remains the highest rank of knighthood in the United Kingdom. The Order's motto is French: 'Honi soit qui mal y pense' – 'Shame on him who thinks ill of it' – and is generally viewed as a statement about Edward's claim to the throne of France.

The Black Death

Edward's early victories were halted by the arrival of the natural disaster that scarred his reign. The Black Death, also known as the Pestilence or the Great Mortality, was a bubonic plague that probably combined with a pneumonic element to make it more deadly. Bubonic plague could be passed in the bites of fleas that had fed on infected rodents. The pneumonic element made it airborne. The plague seems to have emerged in Central Asia and spread quickly along trade routes like the Silk Road. Once it reached the Mediterranean, the merchant ships of Italian city-states helped it spread far and wide. The plague arrived in England on ships in the summer of 1348. Symptoms of the disease began with a fever, aching joints and nausea. Left untreated, sufferers would develop buboes, large black swellings in the neck, armpits or groin. When opened, they contained blood and pus. The fatality rate for those infected has been estimated at around 80%.

From the south coast of England, the plague spread quickly

across the countryside and into towns. With no understanding of germ theory, populations were at a loss to prevent the spread. They also struggled to understand why the Pestilence was being inflicted on them. Anything that the medieval mind could not understand or explain was considered a punishment from God. The only effective way to lift the curse was to reform behaviour, but that required the identification of the fault to be remedied. As the death toll increased, afflicting young and old, rich and poor alike, it was considered a great leveller without an obvious end. The first outbreak in England lasted over a year, but it would return in 1362, 1371, 1382, and sporadically until the last major outbreak in the 17th century. Estimates of the death toll from the early episodes vary widely and are disputed, but it is likely that around half of the populations of affected areas were wiped out. Alongside the devastating loss of loved ones, the social and economic impacts of the Black Death would be felt for

generations, particularly in England after the death of Edward III.

One of Edward's daughters, Joan, died, demonstrating that rank was no protection. King Philip's wife, also named Joan, succumbed too. Philip himself died in 1350 – not of the plague – but, when Edward felt ready to reignite the war with France, he was faced by Philip's son, John II. Now in his early forties, Edward was ably supported by his 25-year-old son and heir the Black Prince. The first surviving use of the Black Prince sobriquet came in the 16th century, though it appears to have been in wide use for some time by then. The meaning of the nickname is unclear. It has been suggested that it may refer to Edward wearing blackened armour and using a black shield, or that it refers to a reputation for brutality. Instances of his cruelty in France are well documented, but historians have posited that they may have been exaggerated or misunderstood.

Edward III arranged alliances to support an invasion of Normandy and sent his son to Gascony to gather support for an assault from the south. The Black Prince arrived in the autumn, at the end of the summer campaigning season, but decided to launch a chevauchée before winter arrived. It was during this period that accusations of the prince's cruelty reached their peak, as he burned and raided across the countryside. When summer arrived in 1356, Prince Edward began to march his army north to join his father's forces in Normandy, raiding as they went. They found their way blocked by French forces and decided to return to Poitiers in Gascony. As they travelled, a French army shadowed them, then overtook them to block their retreat. Some sources claim Edward had around 2,000 men to face 50,000 Frenchmen, though numbers of combatants in medieval battles are notoriously hard to be certain of.

The Battle of Poitiers

The two armies met near Poitiers on 19 September 1356. When the prince was told of the vast French force filling the fields, he replied, 'Well, in the name of God. Let us now study how we shall fight with them to our advantage.' Prince Edward arranged his forces on a ridge near a bend in the River Vienne. It was a solid defensive position that would hamper the French approach. Most of the French dismounted, retaining small cavalry forces designed to harass the English archers. As the forces arrayed for battle, churchmen on both sides tried to negotiate peace. The French demanded the return of all towns and any prisoners they held, along with a promise from all Englishmen on the field not to take up arms against King John for seven years. In response, Prince Edward demanded marriage to the French king's daughter with an eye-watering dowry payment. Neither side really wanted to talk. They were ready for a fight.

As the tension grew, one of the prince's flanks began to withdraw with its baggage train. Spotting the retreat, the French attacked. As soon as they did, the English hurried back into position. The retreat had been a feint to lure the French in, and it had worked. In medieval battles, the general wisdom was that the army that moved first would lose, and the French had been tricked into launching their assault. As the French came closer, the English archers moved to the flanks to shoot in at the cavalry and infantry. The French assault fell into disarray. As King John rallied for a fresh attack, a contingent of English mounted their horses and swung round behind the enemy. The tactic caught the French unawares.

John and his closest companions were Knights of the Order of the Star, an order of chivalry, members of which took a solemn oath never to retreat from a battle. Eventually, King John and his 14-year-old son Philip were surrounded and captured, bringing an end to the Battle of Poitiers and securing the Black Prince's military reputation. John was treated with great respect by the prince, who served the King of France at a feast that evening. When he was taken to London, he was greeted more as an honoured guest than as a prisoner. England had achieved another high watermark in the effort in France. King John spent the next four years as an English captive, though he was well treated. John's son, Dauphin Charles, was left to try to rule France as a regent for his father. Dauphin was a French designation for the heir to the throne, equivalent to the Prince of Wales in England.

Eventually, the Treaty of Brétigny was agreed in 1360. It provided for John's release. England would return some of the lands that had been won but would retain much of its gains around Gascony, effectively enlarging Aquitaine. These lands were to be held clear of any homage to the French king, and the Black Prince would become Prince of Aquitaine. In return, Edward agreed to give up his claim to the French Crown, effectively ending what is known as the Edwardian phase of the Hundred Years' War. John was also required to pay a vast ransom of three million crowns, more than two years of revenue for the French realm. John was released to return home to raise the money after leaving hostages, including two of his sons.

In July 1363, John learned that his son Louis had fled from the English. In a remarkable turn of events, the king gathered his council and announced that he would return to England and submit himself into the English king's custody. He was behind on his ransom payments and found his son's behaviour dishonourable. John arrived in England in January 1364 and was welcomed as a guest. He stayed at Eltham Palace and the Savoy Palace, frequently being entertained by King Edward III personally. John soon fell ill, though, and died in April 1364, aged 44. His body was returned to France to be buried alongside his predecessors at St Denis.

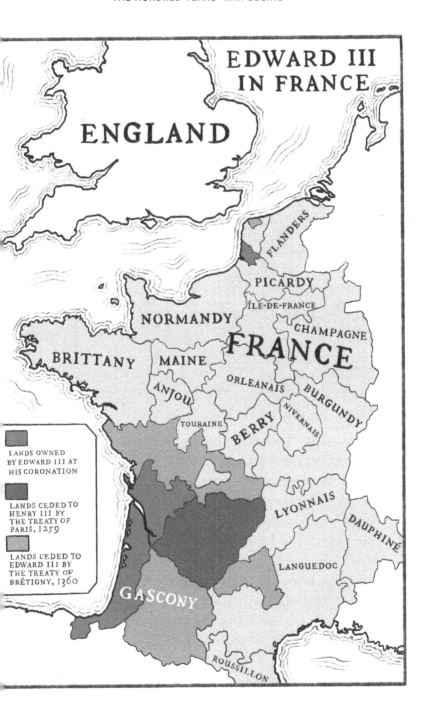

EDWARD III
IN FRANCE

ENGLAND

FLANDERS

PICARDY

ÎLE-DE-FRANCE

NORMANDY

CHAMPAGNE

FRANCE

BRITTANY

MAINE

ANJOU

ORLEANAIS

BURGUNDY

TOURAINE

BERRY

NIVERNAIS

LANDS OWNED
BY EDWARD III AT
HIS CORONATION

LANDS CEDED TO
HENRY III BY
THE TREATY OF
PARIS, 1259

LANDS CEDED TO
EDWARD III BY
THE TREATY OF
BRÉTIGNY, 1360

LYONNAIS

DAUPHINÉ

LANGUEDOC

GASCONY

ROUSSILLON

Despite the prevailing peace, Edward ensured his kingdom remained prepared for war. In 1363, he introduced a new law that required every man to practise with a bow on Sundays and feast days, both stipulated because church attendance was compulsory, so archery practice could happen after church when men were gathered anyway. By this time, Edward had passed his fiftieth birthday and war became increasingly less appealing or likely. The Black Prince became involved in campaigns into the Iberian Peninsula, now Spain and Portugal, following a dispute over the Crown of Castile. He won a victory at the Battle of Nájera on 3 April 1367 that was crushing, but ultimately pyrrhic. Edward III's third son, John of Gaunt, Duke of Lancaster and his fourth, Edmund, Duke of York became embroiled in the conflict in the years that followed. Both married daughters of King Peter of Castile, whom England had favoured in the dispute, and Gaunt would later press a claim to the throne of Castile himself.

LISTEN TO THE
PODCAST

The Hundred
Years' War

In 1371, the Black Prince returned to England and soon afterwards resigned his control of Aquitaine, stating that the income there was insufficient to support the expenditure it required. He was seen as a champion of the reforms many demanded of his father's government. With Edward III increasingly ill, Gaunt, among others, was suspected of driving government corruption for their own ends. The prince sought to help correct this, particularly in a session of Parliament known as the Good Parliament in 1376, which saw several senior officials removed. The prince's own health was becoming problematic, however. He was afflicted by bouts of dysentery; a lifetime spent on military campaigns had taken a toll. On 8 June 1376, Edward, the Black Prince, Prince of Wales and heir to the throne, died aged 45. He was buried at Canterbury Cathedral, where his tomb and effigy, alongside his funerary achievements – his shield, gauntlets and surcoat – symbols of military prowess.

When Edward III's queen Philippa of Hainault died in 1369 after 41 years of marriage, Edward had already become close to a much younger mistress, Alice Perrers. Her influence over Edward was a concern to many around the court. The Good Parliament exiled Alice Perrers as part of its efforts to root out perceived corruption and a large quantity of money and jewels were seized from her as well as the lands she had accumulated. By this time, Edward III had suffered at least one stroke. He was increasingly incapacitated, and government was led by his sons, predominantly John of Gaunt, now the oldest surviving son.

Succeeding Edward III

With the Black Prince's death, the succession was drawn into sharp focus. One chronicler claimed that Gaunt tried to introduce legislation in Parliament that would forbid the transmission of a claim through a female line, but no other account mentions this. A document created in late 1376, but badly damaged by a fire in 1731, sets out Edward's plans. His grandson Richard of Bordeaux, the last remaining son of the Black Prince, would succeed. The next in line would be John of Gaunt. The document passes over Edward III's granddaughter by his second son, seeming to settle succession solely in the male line. Pressure for this move may have come from Gaunt since it moved his family closer to the throne, though it is unclear what legal validity this settlement had.

King Edward III died on 21 June 1377. He was 64 years old and had ruled England for 50 years, coming close to Henry III's record of 56. Edward III had galvanised a kingdom after the divisions of his father's rule and his early years saw notable military success. An accomplished soldier loved by his men and his nobles, Edward used war, first in Scotland, then in France, to bring his realm together. He was also a king interested in culture, and vernacular works by Geoffrey Chaucer and others flourished during his reign. The Order of the Garter reflected Edward's Arthurian interest in creating a brotherhood of elite warriors and remains the highest order of knighthood in the British honours system today.

Although Edward III formally renounced his claim to the French throne in 1360 in the Treaty of Brétigny, English kings would continue to assert that right for centuries to follow. What began as an escalating dispute between Edward III and Philip VI in 1337 would become the Hundred Years' War. English and then British monarchs would maintain their claim to the French Crown until 1802, a decade after it had been abolished during the French Revolution.

As Edward III had set out in his plans, his grandson became King Richard II. Richard was just ten years old. When Henry III had become king at nine, his reign had proven bumpy, and it remained to be seen how Richard's character might develop and how his rule would play out. To have any hope of success, Richard would depend upon the support of his three surviving uncles. John of Gaunt, Edmund and Thomas would have a great deal riding on their shoulders. In the back of their minds the Bible's warning from Ecclesiastes 10:16 might have rumbled: 'Woe to thee, O land, when thy king is a child'.

Chapter 8

Wages, Taxes and Revolution

The minority of Richard II : The Statute of Labourers annoys
the people : Taxation hurts the kingdom : The people of the
countryside rise in protest : The Peasants' Revolt takes London :
The rebels meet the king : The Tower of London is breached :
Richard II becomes a tyrant

R ichard II assumed the throne in 1377 as a ten-year-old heavily dependent on his uncles and those around him. Although boys might marry at 14, and girls at 12, noblemen were not considered to have reached majority and the age when they could take control of their lands until they were 21. The principle had been extended to Henry III, who was declared to have reached his majority by the Pope only in 1228, aged 21. As a result, Richard could expect to remain a minor for the next 11 years.

Richard was born in 1367 to Edward, the Black Prince, and Joan, Countess of Kent. Richard's mother was a granddaughter of Edward I, who lived an eventful and controversial life even before Richard's succession. She was renowned for her beauty and was called the Fair Maid of Kent. Her father was Edmund of Woodstock, the half-brother of Edward II, who had been executed for his part in a plot to free the deposed, and supposedly dead, king in 1330. Joan had been involved in a scandal in the 1340s, when she had secretly married Thomas Holland in 1340 when he was 26 and she was 13. When Holland went to France on campaign immediately afterwards, Joan's family, unaware of her secret union, arranged her marriage to William Montagu, heir to the Earl of Salisbury. Joan would later state that she had not told her family for fear that it might lead to Thomas's execution.

In 1348, Thomas returned from France to find his wife married to another man. He petitioned King Edward III and the Pope to recognise their union, and the following year Pope Clement VI annulled Joan's marriage to William Montagu. Joan and Thomas went on to have five children, four of whom survived infancy. In particular, Richard II's half-brothers, Thomas and John, would play key roles during his reign. After Thomas's death in 1360, Joan married Edward the Black Prince, Richard's father. Edward had shunned the idea of an alternative match with a foreign princess that would bring an international alliance, suggesting that the couple had fallen in love. Joan survived eight years into her son's reign, dying at around sixty years old in 1385.

Given Richard's minority, a perpetual council was set up to govern in the young king's name. It comprised two earls, two barons, two bishops, two knights banneret (a rank above a normal knight, or knight bachelor, who could lead a company into battle beneath his own banner) and four other knights, so that it might represent a broad cross-section (of the upper end) of society.

None of the king's remaining uncles were appointed to the perpetual council. Their position and influence meant that they would have a role in government anyway. John of Gaunt, Duke of Lancaster was the senior adult relative of Richard II, but was by now pressing his claim to the Castilian Crown through his second wife, Constance. He would frequently appear preoccupied and would be accused of diverting funds to his own projects at the expense of resolving England's growing problems. Hangovers from the two major issues of Edward III's reign would mingle to impact the early years of Richard II's, resulting in an unprecedented moment of hope and violence.

The aftermath of the Black Death was still being felt in the late 1370s, 30 years after it first arrived. The plague had wiped out around half the population of England. Estimates put the population at two to three million on Richard's accession; it had been closer to six million before the arrival of the pestilence.

A reduced population across Europe had unexpected consequences. Survivors had been through a terrifying and often

LISTEN TO THE
PODCAST

John of Gaunt

traumatic period of loss, but found themselves in an improved position as the sickness subsided. A drastically reduced labour force saw wages driven upwards. Simultaneously, where there had been famine, there was suddenly plenty, forcing prices down. Those left alive may have inherited land from several relatives who had not been so lucky. Suddenly, they owned more land than they could have dreamt of, could demand higher wages, and were paying less for food than ever before. Villeins, who were unfree, the lowest form of peasants, who lived tied to a piece of land and a lord for whom they worked, could see a chance to break free. For a brief moment, it seemed the pain had left behind some gain. Then the government stepped in.

THE MEDIEVAL CLIMATE

Populations had risen during the Medieval Warm Period, which lasted from the mid-10th century until the mid-13th century. The climate had been optimal for crop growth, facilitating expansion across Europe. When the Medieval Warm Period ended, it was soon replaced by a drastic change in the opposite direction. The Little Ice Age began around 1300 and lasted until the middle of the 19th century. With the end of the Medieval Warm Period, pack ice began to encroach into the North Atlantic regions. From 1315 to 1317, torrential rains caused several years of failed crops and famine. Global temperatures dropped by around 2 °C (3.6 °F) during the period of the Little Ice Age. Rivers would freeze over for weeks in winter. Frost Fairs were held on the River Thames in London, the first event so named in 1608 and the last in 1814.

Political and Religious Crises

In June 1349, as the first outbreak of the plague was still grip-ping England, Edward III's government issued the Ordinance of Labourers. The document complained that 'many seeing the necessity of master, and great scarcity of servants, will not serve unless they may receive excessive wages'. It was clear that the minority elite were panicking and had no intention of losing their grip, or any of their wealth, as a result of the plague. The Ordinances set wages at 1347 levels. Its provisions extended to free peasants too, drawing them closer to their unfree coun-trymen than ever before. In 1351, the provisions were made law when the Statute of Labourers passed through Parliament. The upper wage for jobs was set by statute. Haymaking could pay no more than 1d (1 pence) per day. Mowing was limited to 5d a day. Threshing a quarter (equal to eight bushels, or approximately a quarter of a ton) of wheat or rye could pay no more than 21/2d per day. Threshing a quarter of barley, beans or oats was limited to 11/2d a day. The wages of skilled labourers from carpenters to masons were all limited to pre-pandemic levels.

Punishments for violations of the Statute were extended in 1361 to include imprisonment without bail, a direct violation of Magna Carta that demonstrates the extent of the ongoing problem. Any labourer caught fleeing their job to seek higher wages would be returned, and branded on the forehead with an F for falsehood. The Statute may have been meant as a short-term measure to ensure harvests were gathered in and famine avoided, but repeated visitations of the plague and slow population growth meant that it remained in force. At a local level, law was enforced by sheriffs as the Crown's representatives in the shires, and cases were tried by Justices of the Peace. These judges were not above paying higher wages to ensure their lands were worked while prosecuting neighbours who tried to do the same.

The Church was in crisis during this period too. It was failing to find a solution to God's anger, made clear by the recurring plague. The papacy was in the midst of a schism, when rival Popes each claimed legitimacy. In the early years of Richard II's rule, one Pope sat in Rome while another was based at Avignon in France. The eventual loser in such a rift would be rebranded as an anti-pope. There were growing calls for reform of the Catholic Church. Many wondered how it had become so wealthy and how it owned so much land when Jesus had preached poverty. In England, the reform movement found a champion in John Wycliffe, a priest and professor at Oxford University. Born in Yorkshire, Wycliffe believed that the scriptures were the only way to understand God. The Church's teachings, and its power, were unnecessary. He denounced transubstantiation, the belief that the bread and wine blessed during Mass physically transformed into the body and blood of Christ. He believed requiring confession from Christians was against scripture, and played a part in translating the Bible from Latin into English to make scripture available for the layman.

Wycliffe's call for the reforms of Church corruption garnered support even among the clergy and nobility. John of Gaunt was a notable supporter of the preacher as the Church began efforts to silence Wycliffe. His doctrinal ideas, especially against transubstantiation, saw him move into areas of heresy that cost him a great deal of support. During the summer of 1381, when the many problems facing England collided, Wycliffe and his followers were preaching a popular message against the Church's wealth and authority. By 1382, Wycliffe was facing charges brought by the Church. His remaining support in political circles meant that he was neither excommunicated nor removed from his offices. Wycliffe died in 1384, but his followers, known as Lollards, continued his work. The origin of the term Lollard is obscure,

but it was meant as an insult. The word may derive from a Dutch word for mumbling because Lollards frequently prayed aloud but under their breath. Wycliffe influenced the Czech reformer Jan Hus, who was burned at the stake as a heretic in 1415. Hus is, in turn, viewed as a precursor to Martin Luther, who would drive the Protestant Reformation in the 16th century.

The spark that ignited the problems of 1381 was taxation. Parliament had, for more than a century, granted taxation to the Crown for large projects such as foreign wars. Apart from tithes paid to the Church, there was not regular, annual taxation. When it was levied during the early Hundred Years' War it frequently brought success and wealth, at least to the fighting elite, as a return on investment. Taxes were still the same fractional charges: one-fifteenth of the value of moveable property for those in towns, and one-tenth for those in the countryside. From 1334, the system had been amended slightly. Communities were assessed at a fixed sum based on previous yields and were then free to raise the money however they saw fit. Wealthier individuals might elect to pay more to help their poorer neighbours.

The benefit for the government was certainty about the amount they could expect to raise, which was generally between £37,000 and £38,000.

The assessment had not been updated since 1334. Despite the wage suppression in the aftermath of the Black Death, there was a sense that there was untapped wealth in the kingdom. The Crown began to think of new ways to raise more money from the post-pandemic population as the cost of war in France continued to spiral amid failures. The first experiment was implemented in 1371. The Parish Tax required a fixed sum of 22s 3d from each parish in England. The government was shocked and disappointed by the income generated. The issue was that the government had set the rate based on there being 45,000 parishes in the kingdom. It transpired that there were in fact only 8,500. The amount required from each parish was adjusted to 116s, creating a backlash across the realm. The Parish Tax was never repeated.

The Poll Tax

In January 1377, another innovation was introduced. The Poll Tax seemed like a simple idea. Every man and woman over 14 was required to pay 4d, around a day's wages for a skilled craftsman and two to four days' wages for an unskilled labourer. Each member of the clergy was to pay 4d too. Mendicant friars – those who wandered the countryside preaching and relying on the generosity of others – and genuine beggars were excluded altogether. The tax was a success, raising over £22,000 from the laity alone. The government spotted a potential improvement too. Some of the clergy offered to pay 12d. The flat rate meant that the richest had paid the same as the poorest. If the tax could be staggered, it would raise even more money.

When Richard II's first Parliament met in October of the same year, it was faced with the problems of a minority government and fresh attacks by French ships on the south coast. Necessity caused them to fall back on the old system of fractional tax, but Parliament granted a double subsidy: two-tenths from towns and two-fifteenths from the countryside. Collected in early 1378, it came hard on the heels of the Poll Tax. When Parliament convened in November 1378, it heard that John of Gaunt's campaign against the French threat had been a dismal failure. Gaunt had led an English fleet to St Malo, which sat at the mouth of the River Rance in Brittany. The territory had previously been held by England, and the idea had been to retake it to diffuse French aggression in the Channel. A siege was begun, but the town was stoutly defended by the Breton knight Bertrand du Guesclin, who was known as the Eagle of Brittany, or the Black Dog of Brocéliande, a mythical enchanted forest.

Siege engines pounded the walls of St Malo as Gaunt tried to lure the French outside the walls. The defenders stayed put. When they discovered the English mine approaching the walls, they caused it to collapse. Undermining was a popular siege tactic that aimed to breach a wall or tower in a town or castle. Corners of square towers or where walls changed direction were ideal weak points. If a mine could be dug under the right spot and then collapsed, it could bring the wall down with it. At the siege of Rochester Castle, King John had ordered a mine dug and then packed it with fattened pigs before setting fire to it. The animal fat caused the fire to burn hotter and collapsed the keep wall. At St Malo, the tactic had been countered effectively. Having run out of ideas and money, Gaunt sailed away with his tail between his legs. As the debacle was explained to Parliament, members were furious. All of that tax money had been wasted, and Parliament refused to grant a further round.

By April 1379, Parliament was agreeing to a second Poll Tax.

It was granted with the requirement of access to royal accounts, suggesting they suspected funds were not being used properly. There was increasing concern that Gaunt was using tax money for war with France to fund his efforts in Castile to make himself king. This Poll Tax built on the success of the first. It had 33 layers of taxation rather than a single flat rate. At the top of the list were John of Gaunt and the Duke of Brittany, who were to pay £6 13s 4d each. Earls, widowed countesses and the Mayor of London were assessed at £4. Knights, their widows and London's aldermen were required to pay 40s. Innkeepers were to pay either 2s, 40d or 12d 'according to his estate'. Anyone outside a described category would pay 4d. The clergy were similarly divided into 15 groups. Archbishops were to pay £6 13s 4d, equal to the richest noblemen, down to 4d for the poorest. Only those over 16 were included in the assessment this time, and married couples in the poorest groups could halve their assessment, making one payment instead of two.

Although this round of taxation seemed progressive and promising, it raised just £22,000 from all receipts, less than the first

Poll Tax had gathered just from the laity. Parliament gathered again in January 1380 to hear of more military failures. In reaction, the session disbanded the continual council and declared the 13-year-old Richard II old enough to rule. Parliament decided 'our lord king was now of great discretion and handsome stature; and bearing in mind his age, which was very nearly that of his noble grandfather, whom God absolve, at the time of his coronation'. They somehow overlooked that his grandfather, Edward III, had not ruled himself when he became king. The five principal officers of state, the Chancellor, Treasurer, Keeper of the Privy Seal, Chamberlain and Steward, were appointed to support the king. Simon Sudbury, Archbishop of Canterbury was given the top office of Chancellor.

After this, Parliament agreed to the grant of a fractional tax again, at a rate of one and a half times the usual rate. It was given with the proviso that 'no parliament shall be held within the kingdom which further burdens his poor commons between now and the said feast of Michaelmas in a year's time'. Religious feast days or saints' days were the most popular way of dating events in the medieval Christian world. Michaelmas fell on 29 September 1381, so there was to be no further taxation for at least 18 months. Despite this promise, Parliament was summoned in November 1380 to hear of further failure abroad as the Chancellor announced a staggering £160,000 was needed. Shocked, but recognising the serious threats the kingdom faced, Parliament offered to raise £100,000, two-thirds from the laity and one-third from the clergy. This represented three fractional taxes.

The government decided to try another Poll Tax, but without the complex tiers that had somehow returned less money. A flat rate of 20d or 16d was suggested before 12d was agreed, three times the original levy. There was no married couple's allowance this time, so the poorest who had paid 4d for both members of a couple were now assessed at 12d each, a total of 24d, six times their previous payment. The first two-thirds of the tax was to be delivered by 27 January 1381, meaning that the crippling collections would come in the leanest months of winter. When money began to trickle in, the yield was shockingly low. Some sort of fraud was clear to see. The taxable population recorded in Essex had fallen by 17,000 since the first Poll Tax four years earlier. Kent was missing 13,000 people, Suffolk 27,000, and Norfolk a brazen 30,000. The government was correct. The frequent and increasingly heavy taxation had galvanised communities. They hid poorer families from assessors.

When the government ordered a full reassessment, it was a step too far. People were not used to officials poking their noses into their affairs and their homes. From 1357 to 1371, England had gone 14 years with no taxation from Parliament. Between 1377 and 1381, there were five rounds of harsh, often experimental taxation with nothing to show for them. As the assessors spread out into the countryside, they found resistance that would lead to a summer of violence that almost changed medieval England for ever. Remembered as the Peasants' Revolt, it was called at the time the Great Insurrection, or even the Hurling Time. The word peasant is misleading. Those involved were referred to as rustics, meaning those from the countryside rather than from towns. It does not refer to their social status, and many who became involved were relatively wealthy landowners or skilled craftsmen.

The Great Insurrection

In late May 1381 the tax inspectors rolled into the town of Brentwood, where they had instructed local representatives to gather. As they began to demand more money, Thomas Baker from nearby Fobbing stepped forward and told them the county had paid all it was going to pay. A scuffle broke out, and the inspectors were driven away. Wary of retribution, a meeting was arranged for anyone willing to make a stand on Whitsunday, 2 June. By 4 June, trouble was erupting in Dartford in Kent led by a man named Abel Kerr. In Essex, Wat Tyler would emerge as a leader. Over the days that followed, rebels in various places descended on the homes of landowners, including the Church. They collected and burned records of manorial courts, fines, and anything that proved villein status. These records that kept them in servitude and blacked their path to a better life were targeted throughout the uprising, though violence was also deployed against the people they blamed for their suffering.

On 10 June, the Kentish rebels arrived in Canterbury. They broke open the prisons and got into the archbishop's chambers in the cathedral. Shocked at the riches they found, they are recorded insisting, 'He shall give us account of the revenues of England and of the great profits that he hath gathered since the king's coronation.' The militarised nature of a society that had been at war for almost half a century meant that the groups knew how to organise men, coordinate their actions and send messages, often in code. By 12 June they were converging on Blackheath, a large, open space south of London. It was here that a preacher named John Ball would be recorded giving a famous sermon that included the line, 'When Adam delved and Eve span, who was then the gentleman?'

John Ball was a well-known radical preacher who had been excommunicated. His ideas mirrored those of the rebels. The famous line about Adam and Eve asked where the Biblical precedent for nobility, and servitude, was found. The Church claimed the world was ordered according to God's law, but in the Garden of Eden, paradise on Earth, there were no great lords. John Ball would be tracked down in the aftermath of the Peasants' Revolt, but there is no legal record that associates him with the uprising, or with a sermon at Blackheath. It may be that his ideas were so aligned with those of the rebels that the authorities blamed his preaching for adding to the problems of that summer.

The gathering at Blackheath asked the young king to speak to them. He agreed to meet them at Rotherhithe, halfway between the Tower of London and Blackheath. On the morning of 13 June, Richard was rowed down the Thames in a barge. As they reached Rotherhithe, there was shock on board at the number of people awaiting the king. They had expected a small delegation but found tens of thousands of rebels gathered on the banks. Richard's councillors were made nervous and ordered the barge to turn round. The protestors were furious. Making their way to Southwark, they crossed London Bridge, breaking open more prisons and attacking document stores as they went. London Bridge was a crowded, bustling crossing point. The bridge itself was packed with shops, shrines and homes, teetering high above the narrow roadway.

Once within the city, Londoners came out to join the rebels. The city shared many of their grievances and was a safe haven for villeins fleeing bondage. The crowds made their way to the greatest symbol of all they opposed: the Savoy Palace. Built during Henry III's reign by his wife's uncle, Peter, Count of Savoy, it was now owned by John of Gaunt, the man blamed for squandering so much tax money. Gaunt was in the north at the time, which probably saved his life from the mob. The palace was set ablaze with all of Gaunt's furniture, goods and expensive tapestries inside. All the gold, silver and jewels they could find were thrown into the River Thames. The rebels insisted they were not thieves, though one person would later be charged with stealing £1,000 in cash. Thirty men were trapped in Gaunt's wine cellar by the fire. Their cries were reportedly heard for a week from the smouldering wreck of the Palace, but they were not saved.

As London burned, the king offered to meet the rebels the next day at Mile End. On 14 June, the 14-year-old Richard arrived for the summit. The crowd knelt before him and swore, 'we will not have any other king but you'. He was not the target of their anger, nor was he blamed for the pain they sought to remedy, but he was viewed as the answer to their problems. The king was the source of all law, so the one person who could fix everything for them. Richard asked what the people wanted from him, and Wat Tyler stepped forward to deliver their requests. They wished to see those at the top of government arrested for their actions. Richard agreed, provided they received fair trials. The people wished to be made free, to see the abolition of villein status. Given that many involved were not themselves villeins, it is striking that this was the main thrust of their demands. They also talked of removing the nobility as a link between the king and his people and making each Englishman directly loyal to the king, and the king alone.

To their shock, Richard acquiesced. To a 14-year-old, such potential power seemed like a glittering prize among the ashes

of destruction. He ordered clerks to set up tables and begin producing letters patent to give to everyone confirming their free status. While this was going on, a group returned to London and gained entry to the Tower. The ease with which they got into the fortress suggests they either had support from the guards or, more likely, warrants from the king. Some burst into the apartments of Joan, the king's mother, and demanded kisses from her before they would leave. They then moved on through the White Tower until they found their real prey. Simon Sudbury, the Archbishop of Canterbury and, until his resignation the previous day, Chancellor, as well as Sir Robert Hales, the Treasurer.

With several other men, they were dragged outside and executed, their heads spiked on London Bridge as traitors. The lack of due process, a stipulation of Richard's agreement to their arrests, may have ruined the rebels' cause. John of Gaunt's oldest son Henry Bolingbroke was in the Tower at the time and only escaped by hiding in a cupboard. Although he was only 14, the same age as his cousin the king, hatred of Gaunt may have endangered his life if he had been caught.

Another meeting was arranged between the king and his rebels for the next day, Saturday 15 June, at Smithfield. Now, Wat Tyler presented further demands, including the restoration of Edward I's 1285 Statute of Winchester. What it boiled down to was a request for less interference from central government with life in the shires. Richard cautiously offered to do all he could to help them achieve their aims. All of a sudden, a scuffle broke out. It is unclear whether Tyler spoke too familiarly to the king, or grabbed the reins of Richard's horse, but the Mayor of London, William Walworth, lunged at Tyler and stabbed him with a dagger. Walworth's squire then drew a sword and ran Tyler through.

With their leader dead, the tension at Smithfield instantly climbed. The royal forces were well armed but vastly outnumbered.

There was no way of knowing who would win, but it would be bloody carnage. Suddenly, Richard spurred his horse forward towards the crowds. Making his way into their midst, he called out, 'Sirs, what ails you? You shall have no captain but me: I am your king: be all in rest and peace.' The king's household looked on in dread until the crowd acclaimed their king and began to disperse. Tyler's fate doubtless caused them to realise they had pushed their luck as far as it was safe to go. They had the letters patent that gave them freedom. They quit while they were ahead. To the 14-year-old king, selected by God to rule, wanted by his people as their only lord, and now capable of diffusing an angry mob, it was a moment that swelled his feeling of divine invincibility.

This was by no means the end of the Peasants' Revolt. For weeks and months after the events of June in London, people across England acted on the basis of the letters patent given by Richard. The problem was that those documents were revoked

almost immediately after the rebels left London. Word of this was slow to travel, and people found themselves prosecuted for doing what they believed they were permitted to do. Legal cases erupted across the kingdom as rebels were hunted down and those who had lost documents fought to restore their rights. The long tail of the Peasants' Revolt is often forgotten in the tales of violence from the capital city. Whether Richard approved of the revoking of his promises is uncertain. The direct connection to his people appealed to him, but threatened the lords who currently held the space between them. Parliament sought to undo what the young king had put in place, but Richard caused the session to be asked whether it approved of the reversal as he was still willing to keep his word to the rebels. Unsurprisingly, Parliament was more than happy with the revocation of the king's offers.

One interesting aspect of the uprising that is frequently overlooked is that both men and women joined in. Joanna Ferrour was recorded as taking a key part in the capture of Rochester Castle and was present at Blackheath, and a later criminal indictment named her as the ringleader at the torching of the Savoy, the instigator of the murders of Sudbury and Hales, and the person who stole £1,000 to distribute among her comrades. Joanna and her husband were career criminals but escaped severe punishment. When they got into trouble again in the early 1400s, they came before the king's court only for the monarch to recognise them. He pardoned the couple because they had saved his life as a teenager, helping him hide from the crowds flooding through the Tower on 14 June 1381. How Henry Bolingbroke became King Henry IV is the story of the collapse of Richard II's reign.

LISTEN TO THE
PODCAST

The Peasants' Revolt

The Personal Rule of Richard II: Culture and Tyranny

By 1387, at the age of 20, Richard II was falling foul of an old problem. Many at court believed he had a small group of favourites who were corrupting government for their own enrichment. In November 1386, Parliament gathered to hear of more military failures in France that required additional funds. There was increasing dissatisfaction at the patronage being gathered up by Richard's favourites, and increasing fear that France was about to invade. Richard's demands for money were ignored as the session impeached his Chancellor, Michael de la Pole, Earl of Suffolk, blaming him for the failures of policy. Suffolk was removed, and a council approved by Parliament was forced upon the king. Richard refused to engage with the session and tried to shut it down. He only began to agree to their demands when his uncle Thomas of Woodstock, Duke of Gloucester produced the statute by which Edward II had been deposed and asked his nephew whether he was willing to go the same way as his great-grandfather. This sitting became known as the Wonderful Parliament. The body was increasingly confident in its power as a check on poorly exercised royal power, but Richard had a heightened sense of his divine authority.

The group opposed to the king's faction became known as the Lords Appellant because they entered an appeal of treason against some at Richard's court. Appellant is derived from the Norman French verb *appeler*, to appeal. The group was made up of three magnates: Thomas of Woodstock, Duke of Gloucester; Richard FitzAlan, Earl of Arundel; and Thomas Beauchamp, Earl of Warwick. They were subsequently joined by Henry Bolingbroke, Earl of Derby, and Thomas de Mowbray, Earl of Nottingham. Although they seemed to have achieved their aims of controlling

Richard under the provisions of the Wonderful Parliament, it began to unravel quickly.

Almost immediately, the king ignored the council that had been foisted on him and set about reversing the restrictions placed on him. On 19 December 1387, Richard's cousin Henry Bolingbroke led an army that encountered a force loyal to Richard, under one of his favourites, Robert de Vere, Earl of Oxford. Bolingbroke decisively won the Battle of Radcot Bridge in Oxfordshire, and Richard was forced to agree to summon Parliament again. From February to June 1388, a session known as the Merciless Parliament sat to purge Richard's favourites. Dozens were executed without trial or banished from the kingdom. Two of Richard's favourites, Michael de la Pole and Robert de Vere, had already escaped abroad but were condemned to death in their absence.

With John of Gaunt's return from Spain in 1389, the power of the Lords Appellant was reduced. Richard spent the next decade rebuilding his personal power. His court was famed for its magnificence. The portrait of Richard II that can be found in Westminster Abbey is the earliest known portrait of an English monarch. Richard appears strikingly youthful in the image, as he does on the Wilton Diptych. Created between 1395 and 1399, the diptych is a small, hinged pair of panels with religious images. Despite being around 30 years old, Richard looks childlike as he kneels before the infant Christ, the Virgin Mary, and the angels. At his side are the two English saint-kings, Edmund the Martyr (King of East Anglia 855–869) and Edward the Confessor (King of England 1042–1066), and John the Baptist. The message is clear: Richard is comparing himself to saints, second only in authority to Christ. The first English recipe book, *The Forme of Cury*, emerged from Richard's reign.

High culture could not disguise Richard's political problems. The war with France was still bubbling away, constantly draining funds without any success. Through the 1390s, his rule was considered increasingly tyrannical. He was famed for sitting on his throne on a raised dais and looking down at his court. If the king's eye fell on an individual, they were expected to kneel, avert their gaze, and remain still until the king looked away. Richard had never forgiven the Lords Appellant, and bided his time as he reconstructed his authority. In 1397, he ordered the arrest of his uncle Thomas, Duke of Gloucester. After being taken to Calais to await trial, Thomas was strangled to death in early September 1397, reportedly at Richard's instruction. Richard FitzAlan, Earl of Arundel was tried at Westminster and executed on 21 September 1397. Thomas Beauchamp, Earl of Warwick pleaded guilty and begged for mercy. He was stripped of all of his lands and titles and sentenced to life imprisonment. The three senior Lords Appellant had been removed from the political board.

In 1398, Henry Bolingbroke, Earl of Derby and Thomas de Mowbray, Earl of Norfolk fell out when Henry reported a comment by Thomas that Henry considered treasonous to the king. Richard relished the chance to deal with the two junior Lords Appellant in one fell swoop. He called a trial by combat between them in the East Midlands. With both men in armour and ready to begin, Richard suddenly called the duel off. Perhaps he realised that the winner would survive and be deemed just. Instead, Richard banished both men from the kingdom.

If he felt his problems were over, he would soon be proven wrong.

Chapter 9

The War in France

Richard II is deposed : Henry IV's unsettled reign : Prince Henry
wounded at the Battle of Shrewsbury : Owain Glyndŵr's rebellion :
The Southampton Plot against Henry V : Henry V invades France :
The Battle of Agincourt : The Siege of Rouen : The Dauphin assas-
sinates the Duke of Burgundy : Burgundy joins England : The Treaty
of Troyes is concluded : Henry V's son succeeds, aged nine months

On 3 February 1399, John of Gaunt, Duke of Lancaster died at Leicester Castle at the age of 58. He had been the wealthiest, most powerful man in England after his nephew the king. A controversial figure, he had been targeted by the Peasants' Revolt, accused of diverting tax money to his personal projects in Castile, and had taken a dangerous stance on religious reform in support of John Wycliffe. He had also been one of his nephew's staunchest supporters, though always with one eye on his family succeeding the childless king.

With his uncle's heir Henry Bolingbroke in exile, Richard made what would prove to be the biggest mistake of his life. The king decided to take the Duchy of Lancaster lands into royal hands. This would mean that Richard would become more powerful and wealthier than any king in living memory, just at a time when he was showing himself to be increasingly tyrannical. However, the real problem was the interference it represented in the laws of inheritance. Gaunt had not died a traitor, so his lands were not forfeit to the Crown. His son had the right to inherit. Richard's seizure therefore made everyone with anything to leave to the next generation nervous. Unfortunately for Richard, that was all

HEIRS

An heir presumptive was one who might be next in line, but whose claim could be bettered if, for example, the king had a son. The heir apparent was one whose claim could not be trumped, usually the oldest son of the monarch.

the most powerful men in England. If the king would do this to his own uncle and cousin, what would prevent him from doing it to everyone else?

By upsetting the dynastic apple cart, Richard made those who were growing wary of him panic. When Roger Mortimer, 4th Earl of March died in Ireland acting as the King's Lieutenant there, Richard crossed the narrow sea to try to impose order. Since the Anglo-Norman conquest of Ireland in the 12th century, English kings had maintained a foothold on the island around Dublin. The extent of their true influence waxed and waned, but it never represented full control of Ireland. Roger had been considered by some measures the heir presumptive to Richard II's Crown.

Roger was the great-great-grandson of the Roger Mortimer who had deposed Edward II. Over subsequent generations the family had rebuilt their reputation, until Edmund, 3rd Earl of March married Philippa of Clarence, the daughter of Lionel, Duke of Clarence, who was Edward III's second son. It was Philippa who had been passed over in Edward III's entail, though the validity of that arrangement remained in doubt. Strict primogeniture, and the lack of a bar on the transition of a claim in the female line, could have made the Mortimer family heirs presumptive while Richard lacked a son. Roger left behind two young sons, Edmund and Roger, aged seven and five respectively.

When Richard departed, he left his last living uncle, Edmund, Duke of York as Guardian of the Realm and King's Lieutenant. Once Richard was in Ireland, Henry Bolingbroke returned, landing at Ravenspur in Yorkshire to claim his inheritance. Edmund was caught off-guard, having expected any attack to come from around Dover. He mustered his forces and confronted his nephew Henry at Berkeley in Gloucestershire, but offered no resistance. In fact, he escorted Henry to Bristol. The mood in the country was palpable. Henry had come for his Lancastrian patrimony, but he was increasingly encouraged to take the Crown. He was joined in the north by Henry Percy, Earl of Northumberland and Ralph Neville, Earl of Westmorland, who was married to Henry's half-sister Joan Beaufort. A significant portion of Edmund's army was under the command of John Beaufort, Henry's half-brother. Whatever his feelings, he acquiesced as one nephew sought to depose another.

When Richard had arrived back in Wales, he was at Flint Castle when a delegation arrived to request his abdication. Among those wearing Henry's livery was Edward, the oldest son of the Duke of York. Edward had been created Earl of Rutland and then Duke of Aumale, was considered Richard's closest friend and adviser, and was frequently described by Richard as his brother. Richard's support had disintegrated. He was taken to London and installed in the Tower, where he was presented with the end of his reign. He was asked to resign the Crown in favour of his cousin Henry.

Rise of the House of Lancaster

Parliament was convened on 6 October 1399 at Westminster, judged once more the only forum in which a royal title could be removed and granted to another. A long list of Richard's misdeeds was recounted before Henry claimed the throne. The Mortimer children, in no position to press their own claim, were passed over by a kingdom with no desire for another minority. Henry was crowned King Henry IV, the first king of the House of Lancaster, at Westminster Abbey on 13 October. Richard was moved to Pontefract Castle. A group of his supporters planned to free him in a plot known as the Epiphany Rising. It failed, but, in line with the story of Edward II, it highlighted the danger of a deposed king remaining alive. Richard was reported to have died around 14 February 1400, possibly starved to death to avoid leaving marks on his body. As with Edward II, rumours persisted that Richard II remained alive for many years after his demise was reported.

Henry IV's reign was dogged by revolts. In September 1400, when he had been king for less than a year, a Welsh landowner descended from old local royalty began a rebellion. Owain Glyndŵr, proclaimed Prince of Wales, held a parliament at Machynlleth and seeking independence from England. He became allied with Henry Percy, Earl of Northumberland and Sir Edmund Mortimer. Percy had become disaffected with Henry IV after failing to receive the rewards he felt his support had warranted. Sir Edmund Mortimer was the uncle of young Edmund and Roger Mortimer. He had been captured at the Battle of Bryn Glas in 1402 fighting against

LISTEN TO THE
PODCAST

The Origins
of Treason

Glyndŵr. Henry had refused to pay Edmund's ransom, perhaps pleased to be rid of a Mortimer who might prove a rival. Sir Edmund defected to Glyndŵr's cause in response, and married one of Owain's daughters.

In 1403 Northumberland and his brother Thomas, Earl of Worcester renounced their fealty to Henry IV. Sir Edmund was Northumberland's son-in-law, and the failure to pay his ransom was added to their grievances. Northumberland's son, Henry Percy, nicknamed Hotspur for his keenness to rush into battle, led an army with Thomas towards Wales to join Glyndŵr, against whom they had previously fought. Henry IV intercepted them at Shrewsbury and, on 21 July 1403, the Battle of Shrewsbury saw a crushing royal victory. Hotspur was killed in the fighting. His nickname is the root of the name of Tottenham Hotspur Football Club, whose original stadium was built on land donated by the Percy family. The club badge of a cockerel with spurs is also Hotspur's motif.

Henry IV's oldest son, another Henry, fought in the battle aged 16. At some point, he raised the visor on his helmet, and was struck in the cheek by an arrow. It was lodged six inches into his face. The shaft was pulled out, but the arrowhead remained buried in the wound. After the battle, Henry was taken to Kenilworth Castle in the East Midlands for treatment. A surgeon named John Bradmore was tasked with removing the arrow. He created a special tool for the job, which he described in his account of treating the injury.

First, I made small probes from the pith of an elder, well dried and well stitched in purified linen [made to] the length of the wound. These probes were infused with rose honey. And after that, I made larger and longer probes, and so I continued to always enlarge these probes until I had the width and depth of the wound as I wished it. And after the wound was as enlarged and deep enough so that, by my reckoning, the probes reached the bottom of the wound, I prepared anew some little tongs, small and hollow, and with the width of an arrow. A screw ran through the middle of the tongs, whose ends were well rounded both on the inside and outside, and even the end of the screw, which was entered into the middle, was well rounded overall in the way of a screw, so that it should grip better and more strongly.

The ingenious surgeon tells how he washed the wound with white wine and wiped the inside of it out with a probe covered with honey, an early antiseptic, barley, flour and flax. Bradmore cleaned the wound in this way for the next 20 days, each day making the probe a little smaller to allow the wound to heal as it was cleansed. To prevent seizures, a possibility that obviously concerned Bradmore, he applied medicines to the prince's neck to loosen the muscles. Bradmore saved the prince's life, but Henry was left scarred. The mark has been offered as an explanation for why Henry's portrait as king was created in profile, to hide the scar.

In 1405, the Tripartite Indenture was negotiated between Owain, Northumberland and Sir Edmund Mortimer. It sought to split England and Wales into three. Glyndŵr would rule Wales, Percy the north of England and young Edmund Mortimer, 5th Earl of March the remainder. It was envisaged as a permanent partition with provision for each man's heirs to inherit. Edmund Mortimer was abducted from Windsor Castle to facilitate the plan, but he was quickly recovered and placed in tighter custody. Glyndŵr forged an alliance with France that saw French forces land in Wales to support his uprising in 1405, though they had little impact. As England and France sought peace,

LISTEN TO THE
PODCAST

King Henry V

Charles VI of France withdrew his support for an independent Wales.

Owain penned the Pennal Letter in 1406, named for the small village near Machynlleth where it was written. It was addressed to Charles VI and asked for continued military support. Owain set out his vision for an independent Wales, with its own parliament, a separate Welsh Church, and two universities. He sought a return to old Welsh laws – the law of Hywel Dda, a 10th-century ruler – to replace the English law enforced at Edward I's conquest. Glyndŵr's rebellion would remain active until 1412, when he vanished. His final fate is unknown, though one Welsh chronicler reported that he died in 1415 after several years in hiding.

Henry IV had gained a strong military reputation by the time he became king. He had spent time crusading in the Baltic with the Teutonic Knights. As king, he survived all of the threats against him, though their persistence prevented him from engaging in the pursuit of war with France. From 1405 onwards, his health became a serious and recurring problem. Henry suffered from a skin disease, which may have been psoriasis or a form of leprosy. Contemporaries suggested his afflictions were a punishment from God for his execution of Richard Scrope, Archbishop of York as part of the rebellions in 1405. As Henry's health failed, his son Prince Henry took an increasing role in government. The king lingered for many years. There were later stories of a prophecy, repeated by Shakespeare, that Henry would die in Jerusalem. On 20 March 1413 Henry died, aged 45, in the Jerusalem Chamber at Westminster Abbey. He had overseen 14 years of trouble and revolt that hinged on his seizure of the throne from his cousin in 1399.

Re-eruption of the Hundred Years' War

Henry V was crowned on 9 April 1413 aged 26. He had seen his father's rule stumble and immediately set about securing the throne by reuniting the nation. Henry V shared with his great-grandfather Edward III the ability to galvanise and inspire men. He returned lands to those who had opposed his father. The Mortimer boys, now adults who had spent the last few years in Henry's household, were freed in 1413. Edmund Mortimer, 5th Earl of March became one of the wealthiest landowners in England. Henry was willing to draw threats close to him rather than pushing them away, further into opposition. When faced with dissent, Henry could be ruthless. He pursued Lollards, the followers of Wycliffe's reforms, as heretics. A Lollard uprising in January 1414 led by Sir John Oldcastle saw Oldcastle and a number of others burned at the stake.

The main policy that Henry employed to create unity was the reignition of the war with France. He bet on the opportunity for glory and riches galvanising any remaining uncertainty. Victory in battle in France would be the finest way to demonstrate God's favour of Lancastrian kingship too. Henry began preparations for an invasion as soon as he became king. His efforts were in part funded by Richard Whittington, Mayor of London.

Henry's decision was informed by France's vulnerability when he came to the throne. Charles VI was the grandson of John II, who had been England's prisoner

THE REAL DICK WHITTINGTON

Richard Whittington served several terms as mayor. He grew incredibly wealthy and left his fortune to charity to do good work in London. The foundation still exists and distributes millions of pounds in funds today. Despite this, he is best remembered as the inspiration for the pantomime character Dick Whittington.

in the previous century. He had ruled France since 1380, when he was 12 years old. Now in his late forties, his reign had been dogged by intermittent but serious mental health issues. Charles had regular breakdowns, during which his symptoms ranged from refusing to wash or change clothes, to failing to recognise his wife and children, and extended to attacking courtiers who came too close because he believed he was made of glass and would shatter. Regencies under his uncles or his wife had become common. France must have appeared weak and open to attack. Henry wrote to Charles, inviting him to hand over the Crown to avoid unnecessary bloodshed. It was a nicety that might begin building Henry's excuses for making war, but he cannot have believed Charles would agree.

LISTEN TO THE
PODCAST

The Real Dick
Whittington

As Henry gathered his army and fleet at Southampton in 1415, a plot was exposed to him. The plan was reportedly to assassinate Henry and his brothers and make Edmund Mortimer king in his place. The leader of what became known as the Southampton Plot was Richard of Conisburgh, Earl of Cambridge. Richard was the youngest son of Edmund, Duke of York and brother to Edward, the present duke. Richard had only been created Earl of Cambridge the previous year, and the revolt must have felt like a poor repayment. Cambridge and two other conspirators, Henry, Lord Scrope of Masham and Sir Thomas Grey of Castle Heaton, were tried alongside Cambridge. All three were executed in early August.

On 12 August 1415, Henry embarked on his invasion. His forces laid siege to the port town of Harfleur, which fell on 22 September. Henry decided to march his army across land to Calais, still held by the English, despite warnings from his council that it was an unnecessarily long and dangerous route. A French army shadowed them as they travelled. If Henry wanted a fight, a chance to prove himself and his claim to the English Crown, he was succeeding in provoking and taunting the French. He offered single combat to the Dauphin, the king's oldest son, to settle the matter one-on-one. The Dauphin declined.

The English force had lost men at the Siege of Harfleur, some being invalided home. Dysentery, the old enemy of campaigning armies, was ripping through the group that marched towards Calais. Henry had between 6,000 and 8,000 men, the majority archers. The French army was at least double, perhaps triple that size. Eventually, both sides agreed to give battle. Henry managed to select the terrain, and used it to his advantage, choosing a narrow field between two wooded areas that would funnel the French forces and help negate their numbers. Freshly ploughed, the churned earth would also hinder cavalry, and when it rained all night the mud only improved English chances.

The Battle of Agincourt

On 25 October 1415, St Crispin's Day, the Battle of Agincourt began near the small town of Azincourt, the name of which would become anglicised. Both sides were conscious of the accepted truth that the army that moved first would usually lose a battle. The French had time and supplies on their side. They could afford to simply wait for the hungry, sick English army to be forced to act. Henry arranged his army with the archers among the smaller contingent of men-at-arms, as English armies had in France for almost a century. Overnight, he had ordered his men to gather wooden stakes and to sharpen both ends. One point was hammered into the mud so that the other faced the increasingly restless French cavalry. Charles VI was not with his force. It was nominally led by his inexperienced son the Dauphin, but the flower of French chivalry and the greatest lords in the land were jostling for control, believing glory was imminent.

As the French waited, it was the English who felt time pressing. As the enemy squabbled, Henry ordered his archers to pull up their stakes and move them forward, into longbow range. Had the French cavalry spotted the manoeuvre, they could have charged. Even allowing for the muddy ground, the English forces were unprotected and preoccupied. On such moments the fate of kingdoms might hang. Distracted by their own debates, the French missed the opportunity. The English drove their stakes back into the soft earth and retreated behind the cover they provided. As the archers nocked their arrows, it was too late. One source describes the English army suffering so badly with dysentery that archers cut the back out of their hose and were forced to endure the diarrhoea where they stood. A medieval longbowman would be expected to loose around eight arrows a minute, with some achieving as much as twelve. If Henry had around 5,000 archers, he could expect them to fill the sky with around 50,000 arrows a minute if they maintained a steady rate.

Under this bombardment, and unable to move back through the mass of their own ranks, the French vanguard took the chance to launch a charge. The cloying mud made the going almost impossible. The spikes prevented the horses getting near to the

English forces, and the archers began firing flat, picking targets rather than launching clouds of arrows. Horses were driven wild as their flesh was pierced. Knights thrown to the ground were sucked into the mud and trampled by panicked steeds. As archers ran out of arrows, they began supporting the men-at-arms. Using their daggers or the mallets that had driven their stakes into the ground, they dashed out to deliver the *coup de grâce*, the killing blow, to fallen knights. This was usually done with a dagger through the slit in a helmet, through the eye and into the brain.

The French fell into the old trap of relentlessly pressing forward, confident that the prowess of their knights and the weight of their numbers would prevail. Retreat was not an option, not on French soil against an inferior force. The field grew impossible to manoeuvre in as English soldiers clambered around the tangle of bodies, killing those who had fallen and dragging down those unable to move their horses. Casualties among the French climbed. For the English, the losses were low. The vanguard was led by Edward, Duke of York. He had pleaded for the honour in the wake of his little brother's treason at Southampton and would be the highest-ranking English casualty at Agincourt. Another nobleman who fell was the 21-year-old Michael de la Pole, 3rd Earl of Suffolk. His father had been killed at the Siege of Harfleur and he had held his earldom for just over a month. York's titles would pass to his nephew, Richard, Duke of York. The Suffolk title went to Michael's brother William. Both men would have a tremendous impact on English politics over the decades that followed.

A moment of controversy came for Henry when news reached him of French reinforcements approaching the rear of his army, where the baggage train and the prisoners were gathered. Concerned that the captured French knights could rearm and join the assault, Henry ordered the killing of the prisoners. Sources are unclear about whether this was actioned, or how many might have been put to death before it became clear the news was incorrect. What Henry did was within the accepted rules of war. Prisoners could be killed to prevent them rejoining the fight, or if they posed a significant danger to Henry's own men. His primary concern was supposed to be the lives of his soldiers. No contemporary English or French source criticised the order. French sources blamed their own commanders for their terrible organisation. However, over the centuries that have followed, Henry has been accused of an unforgivable war crime at Agincourt.

Agincourt was a victory against the odds, but one in a line of similar wins for English tactics on French soil. When the exhausted English force made it to Calais and returned to England, Henry was welcomed as a conquering hero with pageants in the streets of London. He wasted little time in laying the plans to capitalise on his victory. The French nobles and knights captured at Agincourt represented some of the cream of French politics and chivalry, which left the enemy significantly weakened. Among dozens of prisoners were Charles, Duke of Orleans, a nephew of Charles VI.

He would remain a prisoner in England for 25 years, becoming a prolific poet. Another captive was Jean le Maingre, known as Marshal Boucicaut. The Marshal of France, he was a famed knight considered one of the finest fighting men in Europe.

Keen to make the most of the situation, Henry returned to France. In 1417 he captured the Norman city of Caen as he sought to conquer and retain territory systematically. The ancient links between Normandy and England made the duchy an appealing target. On 5 August 1417, four days after his arrival in France, Henry took a striking step. He began to issue royal warrants from the Chancery in English, and there was a considered move away from French as a language of government. At the very time Henry was seeking to unite the two Crowns, he reinforced the divisions between the realms in the most obvious terms possible: language. Henry was calling to a sense of Englishness, even among the elite that had once considered themselves more French than English. Henry III's reign had seen the emergence of a more English identity among a noble class cut off from their ancestral lands on the Continent. Edward III's war had galvanised that idea. Now, there were to be no blurred lines, no division between the nobility and the people. They were all English, and all united in a fight against a common enemy. Englishness was weaponised to other the French.

In 1418, Henry invested the Siege of Rouen, the Norman capital. As the blockade stretched into the bitter winter months, another moment of controversy arrived for Henry. Those within Rouen gathered their elderly, women and children and pushed them outside the city gates. Their intention was to make the supplies within the city last longer. Henry refused to allow those ejected to pass the English blockade. What the French had done was outside the well-established rules of siege warfare. They hoped to prolong the siege, which Henry could not allow.

The vulnerable of Rouen were trapped against the city walls.

They began to starve to death, and to freeze as temperatures plummeted. Those within were forced to listen to the cries of their fellow citizens and watch them die. Still, they were refused entry or passage. Like the order to kill prisoners at Agincourt, this moment has seen Henry accused of vicious cruelty. Those within Rouen's walls were at least as cruel, if not more so, since they watched friends and neighbours suffer. Henry V was undoubtedly ruthless. His aim was to shorten the siege, not allow it to be prolonged. These incidents have led to Henry's reputation becoming polarised. On the one hand is the victor of Agincourt, whose greatest moment was yet to come. On the other is a man who ordered the killing of prisoners and allowed women, children and vulnerable citizens of Rouen to starve and freeze to death.

Rouen fell on 19 January 1419. On 10 September, an unexpected turn of events swung the war in England's favour. The ongoing mental illness of Charles VI created tensions in France as factions jostled for control of the government. The two primary rivals were the followers of the Duke of Orleans and those of the

Duke of Burgundy. Efforts to reconcile the parties had failed and on 23 November 1407 Louis, Duke of Orleans was brutally assassinated in the streets of Paris. Suspicion immediately fell on John, Duke of Burgundy, known as John the Fearless. To the surprise of many, John freely admitted that he had ordered the killing, claiming he was doing France a favour by ridding it of a tyrant. Incredibly, John suffered no sanction for his brazen crime.

Louis's son became Duke of Orleans aged 14 and was guided by his father-in-law the Count of Armagnac, leading to his faction becoming known as the Armagnacs. When the new Duke of Orleans was captured at Agincourt, John was emboldened and in May 1418 moved to take control of the city of Paris. From here, he failed to oppose the Siege of Rouen. The Dauphin Charles, the heir to the throne, became a figurehead for the Armagnac faction, and, as Henry took increasing control of northern France, there was a fresh effort to reconcile the parties.

The Treaty of Troyes

On 10 September 1419, with Henry moving towards Paris, the Dauphin met John on a bridge at Montereau for peace talks during which one of Charles's men murdered the duke. John's son, Philip II, nicknamed Philip the Good, immediately sought an alliance with Henry in order to seek vengeance for his father's death. During the 16th century, a monk was reported showing the skull of John the Fearless to King Francis I and remarking that the hole made by the weapon that killed him was the breach through which the English were able to enter France. The Dauphin's rash actions in revenge for the murder of Louis, Duke of Orleans placed the Crown to which he was heir in serious peril.

Six months of negotiations followed. The result of the talks was the Treaty of Troyes, an unparalleled high point in England's

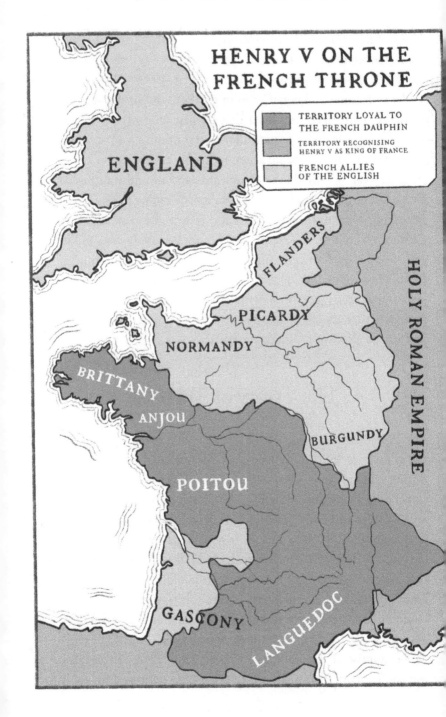

HENRY V ON THE FRENCH THRONE

TERRITORY LOYAL TO
THE FRENCH DAUPHIN

TERRITORY RECOGNISING
HENRY V AS KING OF FRANCE

FRENCH ALLIES
OF THE ENGLISH

ENGLAND

HOLY ROMAN EMPIRE

FLANDERS

PICARDY

NORMANDY

BRITTANY

ANJOU

BURGUNDY

POITOU

GASCONY

LANGUEDOC

efforts to win the French Crown, agreed on 21 May 1420. Henry was married to the youngest daughter of King Charles, Catherine of Valois. Moreover, the King of England and his heirs were recognised as heirs to the throne of France in succession to Charles VI, who would remain king for the remainder of his life. Henry was appointed regent of France, to run the government in the meantime. The Dauphin Charles was completely disinherited, as a mark of his father's dislike of his actions but also in recognition of Henry's momentum. Later in 1420, the French Estates-General approved the Treaty of Troyes as Henry entered Paris. The Estates-General was an advisory body, similar to Parliament in England but without any real authority, and no power, for example, to grant or refuse taxation.

As Henry returned to England with his new wife, his oldest brother Thomas, Duke of Clarence took command in France. On 22 March 1421, Thomas led an army against an alliance of French and Scottish forces at the Battle of Baugé but suffered a crushing defeat, during which Thomas was killed. Henry returned to France in the aftermath of his brother's death, and by May 1422 had captured the towns of Dreux and Meaux. Henry, who may have contracted dysentery in the aftermath of the Siege of Meaux, became ill during the summer. Although he rallied for a while, his health collapsed in August. At the age of thirty-five, and after nine years as king, Henry had attained what his great-grandfather Edward III had not. His brief stay in England after his marriage had resulted in the birth of a son, another Henry. The king was forced to reflect that, like his great-grandfather, he would be succeeded by a child with a long minority before him, and before England.

Henry wrote a new will as he ailed. He left his oldest remaining brother John, Duke of Bedford to act as Regent of France. His youngest brother Humphrey, Duke of Gloucester was to be Regent of England, though was to relinquish the role to John whenever he was in England. Instructions were included regarding prisoners taken at Agincourt. Charles, Duke of Orleans was not to be released; as he was leader of the Armagnac faction, it would risk revitalising England's chief opponents in France. Having laid plans for his son's long minority as best he could, Henry V died on 31 August 1422 at Château de Vincennes. Even as his body was being returned to England for burial at Westminster Abbey, his plans were being undone.

There was little issue with John, Duke of Bedford acting as regent in France. However, the body politic in England did not wish for a regency there. There was concern about focussing power in the hands of one person, and Humphrey, Duke of Gloucester was considered particularly unsuitable. Although regencies in France were commonplace, England had never taken to the idea. Humphrey was a learned man, an early Renaissance figure whose collection of books formed the basis of the Bodleian Library at Oxford, but he was also a rash and bellicose character. Behind the concern was a fear that members of the nobility might miss out on power and authority during a minority. A new plan was made for England.

A tripartite separation of power was created. Council would govern England in the name of the infant king. A new office was invented for Humphrey. He would be Lord Protector of the Realm. The post would have responsibility for internal and external military security, and Humphrey would be given a seat on the council, but not a controlling one. The third part of the

arrangement was that the person of the king would be placed into the care of a tutor who would be responsible for his upbringing and education.

Henry V died at the height of his powers. Without time to fail, he became remembered as a hero, though his reputation was made problematic by concerns about his harsher actions in France and whether he committed war crimes. The Treaty of Troyes represented a new moment in the Hundred Years' War, with the English king and his successors recognised by France as heirs to its Crown. Charles VI died on 21 October 1422, less than eight weeks after his son-in-law. Had Henry lived longer, the history of Western Europe might have been very different. Two kingdoms waited with bated breath for the end of the minority of King Henry VI of England.

Chapter 10

The English Kingdom
of France

The Duke of Bedford acts as Regent of France : The Battle of
Verneuil : The arrival of Joan of Arc : The Battle of Patay :
The coronations of Charles VII and Henry VI : The capture of Joan
of Arc : Joan's trial and execution : Burgundy allies with Charles VII :
The death of John, Duke of Bedford

E ngland had a long wait ahead until little Henry VI might be ready to pick up his father's mantle and pursue his claim to the Crown of France. Legally, on the death of Charles VI on 21 October 1422, the infant Henry became King of France. Making that office a reality in the face of a minority and revitalised Armagnac opposition led by Dauphin Charles, who now styled himself King Charles VII, was a different matter.

The fighting in France continued under the command of John, Duke of Bedford. On 31 July 1423, the English won at the Battle of Cravant, where they faced a French and Scots army. During the fighting French forces retreated, but the Scots refused to do so. As many as 3,000 may have been killed trying to oppose the English. Their leader, Sir John Stewart of Darnley, lost an eye and was captured. Although the English had won some of the most famous victories of the Hundred Years' War, they had frequently lost engagements too. At the Battle of La Brossinière on 26 September 1423, an English army led by John de la Pole, brother of William, Earl of Suffolk, was crushed and its commanders captured.

The Battle of Verneuil on 17 August 1424 became known as the second Agincourt. Around 8,000 English troops faced up to 16,000 French soldiers on the southern border of Normandy. Although John, Duke of Bedford, who led the English army, claimed he only lost two men-at-arms and a few archers, other estimates suggest his losses were closer to 1,600. The French were reported as losing up to 6,000 men. A Milanese cavalry force managed to press through the bombardment of arrows and breach the stakes arrayed by the archers, routing one wing. The riders pursued the archers from the field and began looting the baggage train.

When the archers who had fled returned, they found fierce hand-to-hand combat among the men-at-arms and threw themselves back into the fray. The French eventually realised that they could not win and withdrew, but the large Scots contingent once more refused to back down. They were eventually surrounded and overwhelmed by Bedford's forces. Of the casualties on the French side, around 4,000 were Scots. Among them was the Earl of Buchan, who had been appointed Constable of France, placing him in command of the French military. Verneuil repeated the crushing Agincourt victory for the English, and the Scots army's part in the Hundred Years' War was effectively ended, though many Scotsmen remained in France to continue to fight.

In October 1428, the Siege of Orleans began. As the seat of the Duke of Orleans, it represented a significant target as the English pressed south to squeeze the Armagnacs out. The siege was conducted by William de la Pole, Earl of Suffolk, and John Talbot, a renowned general. It spilled into the next year and an engagement took place on 12 February 1429 that became known as the Battle of the Herrings. A French force led by Charles, son of the Duke of Bourbon, and Sir John Stewart, who had been freed since the Battle of Cravant, tried to ambush an English supply train under the care of Sir John Fastolf, a knight quickly making himself famous and wealthy in France. The French forces reportedly numbered around 4,000 against the 1,600 Englishmen, but Fastolf was able to lead his men to victory. The wagons they protected contained crossbow shafts, cannons and cannonballs for the siege at Orleans, but also barrels of herrings to feed the besiegers. It is for these that the battle was given its name.

The Maid of Orleans

It was now that a turning point arrived. A young girl now remembered as Joan of Arc began to claim she was receiving visions from the Archangel Michael and others ordering her to support the Dauphin and to see him crowned as the rightful King of France. When Joan eventually reached the royal court in March 1429, Charles was sceptical. His dilemma was in trying to determine whether Joan was a prophetess sent to bless his cause or a witch who would damn his soul. He arranged a line-up and asked her to be brought into the room to pick him out from among his courtiers. Joan spotted him immediately. She was then sent to Charles's mother to be examined by a group of women, who confirmed she was a virgin, before a panel of theologians cautiously offered that they could see no heresy in her words.

Joan told Charles she would lift the siege at Orleans, which had been going on for half a year, then get him crowned. Despite still being unsure, Charles gave Joan armour, a sword and an army and sent her to Orleans. On 8 May 1429, nine days after Joan's arrival, the English fled from Orleans, and the siege was broken. Joan marched her army through the Loire Valley toward Reims, the traditional location for the coronation of French kings. On 11 June, they arrived outside the town of Jargeau and laid siege to the English inside. On the next day, an assault on the town included the use of cannons as Joan led an attack. The French swept to victory at the Battle of Jargeau. The English suffered heavy casualties, though their commander William de la Pole, Earl of Suffolk escaped. Joan had won her first offensive victory, and pressed on.

LISTEN TO THE
PODCAST

Joan of Arc

At the Battle of Meung-sur-Loire on 15

June, the English, under John Talbot, were defeated. The town controlled a bridge over the River Loire that gave the French access to the north and hampered English manoeuvres. Joan's forces swiftly moved on to Beaugency, another critical river crossing, arriving on 16 June. The English, under Talbot once again, retreated within the castle, and the French forces began to pound the walls with cannon fire. The next day, the French offered the English the opportunity to surrender with safe conduct. Having seen the slaughter of their comrades at Jargeau and Meung-sur-Loire, they readily agreed. The French keenness to end the siege lay in the news that English reinforcements were due to arrive, something those inside the castle were unaware of.

Encouraged by their quick and apparently easy success, French confidence grew rapidly. The climax of Joan of Arc's Loire campaign came on 18 June 1429 at the Battle of Patay. John Talbot prepared in what was now the traditional English way, arranging his longbowmen, the majority of his force, behind a line of stakes to wait for the French cavalry charge. A group of archers were sent along the road to prepare an ambush for the French, but gave their position away when they spotted a stag. Failing to realise how close the French were, they sent up a hunting call. The ambush was ruined, and the unprotected archers were cut down by the cavalry. Their removal left the English flank open, and the French knights took full advantage, charging into the side of the English army. Another group of French cavalry circled around to attack from the rear, and the English force was trapped between hammer and anvil.

English casualties were high. John Talbot, Thomas, Baron Scales and Sir Thomas Rempston were among the commanders captured, though Sir John Fastolf and his small cavalry force were able to escape the field. Patay was a crushing defeat for the English in France, the conclusion of the Loire campaign that had seen lightning strikes re-energise the French as each victory increased their morale. As the English withdrew to Paris, Joan was delivering what she had promised Charles and what God had instructed her to do. On 17 July 1429, Charles was crowned King of France at Reims Cathedral. In four months, a young girl had inspired a nation that had been in the doldrums for at least all her life. After generations of success, English tactics were beginning to fail as the French invested in gunpowder weapons. Some adaptation to this new reality would be required if the French advances were to be halted.

The loss at Patay had two more consequences. Sir John Fastolf was accused of cowardice for fleeing the field. Contemporary French chroniclers offered no censure for his withdrawal but understood that the English viewed it as dishonourable. In Paris, John, Duke of Bedford suspended Fastolf from the Order of the Garter. Approaching 50, Fastolf had been in France since 1415. He had missed Agincourt after falling ill at the Siege of Harfleur but had grown wealthy and famous in the wars in France. At the Siege of Orleans, Joan of Arc responded to news that English reinforcements were on the way by warning a colleague, 'in the name of God I command you that as soon as you hear of Fastolf's coming, you will let me know. For if he gets through without my knowing it, I swear to you that I will have your head cut off.' The Order of the Garter was England's premier chivalric club. It had no statute against leaving a battlefield nor to allow suspension from the Order, but Bedford reacted to the public concern at the loss by making Fastolf a scapegoat.

Sir John continued in high office, defending Paris and leading armies in the field. When John Talbot was released from captivity in 1433, four years after Patay, he furiously reignited the accusations of cowardice, and pursued Fastolf for years. Talbot may have felt embarrassed at his own failure and lashed out at Fastolf, but it became a long-running feud. The matter was only brought to a close in 1442. Possibly at Fastolf's insistence, an inquiry was

launched by the Order of the Garter into the accusations against him. Fastolf was eventually found innocent of any cowardice or wrongdoing and reinstated to the Order, though his reputation had been seriously damaged. In the same year, John Talbot was created Earl of Shrewsbury in recognition of his work in France, but perhaps also to take the sting out of his feud with Fastolf. Sir John Fastolf died in England in late 1459, a wealthy man who had built Caister Castle. He died the day before his seventy-ninth birthday, a fine age for a man embroiled in war for most of his adult life.

The Coronations of Henry VI

The other significant reaction from the English was to arrange the coronation of their own King of France. In 1429, Henry VI was approaching his eighth birthday. Bedford believed a coronation in France would take the sting out of Charles VII's new position. In England, there was concern that he ought to be crowned there first, to ensure that the English Crown had seniority. One of the questions that had never been answered throughout the Hundred Years' War was how the kingdoms might be ruled. France was much larger and richer than England, which feared becoming the junior partner in a new landscape that saw its king evacuate London in favour of Paris. Henry would not be allowed to travel to France until he was properly crowned as King of England.

On 6 November 1429, a month before his eighth birthday, the boy was taken to Westminster Abbey to undergo the most solemn of religious rites. The delay in crowning him may have been, in part, due to some requirement that he should understand what was happening. Henry III's provision for succession meant that Henry was the legitimate king, even uncrowned. In addition, there may have been caution after the experiences of Richard II's reign, when exposure to notions of being selected by God had affected the man the boy had become. With France resurgent, Bedford concluded there was no more time to waste.

The coronation began with the Recognition, the Archbishop of Canterbury still asking for the approval of the congregation almost 400 years after the abolition of any form of elective element. To shouts of 'Ye! Ye!', the boy was led before the altar, where he lay prostrate on the floor. After prayers had been said around him, he was anointed with holy oil before being re-dressed in scarlet gowns edged with ermine. He was handed pieces of regalia, and then St Edward's Crown was perched on top of his small head.

The service was followed by the coronation banquet, a tradition which endured until William IV did away with it due to the cost. The king's champion rode into the hall and offered a challenge to anyone who doubted the king's rights. When no one took up the challenge, he was ceremonially handed a jewelled cup of wine. After taking a sip, he threw the rest on the floor and kept the cup as his payment. At the top table sat a bishop from France, offering a nod to the novelty of Henry's new dual monarchy.

After the coronation, Parliament oversaw the ending of the role of the Protector. Henry's uncle Humphrey, Duke of Gloucester was removed from office, though his other uncle, Bedford, retained his post in France. Attention began to turn to the practicalities of getting the young king crowned in France. It was decided that his great-uncle, Cardinal Henry Beaufort, Bishop of Winchester, should be sent ahead to lay the groundwork. Beaufort was the last surviving son of John of Gaunt from his relationship with Katherine Swynford. His sister, Joan Beaufort, was also still alive and was matriarch to a large brood as the wife of Ralph Neville, Earl of Westmorland. As Bishop of Winchester, Cardinal Beaufort was the wealthiest bishop in England. He helped fund the English efforts in France and would seek the promotion of his Beaufort nephews as compensation.

There was no shortage of noblemen seeking to escort the king to France. It was a prestigious moment to accompany a king when he travelled overseas, but the chance to watch the first coronation in history of a King of England as King of France exerted a deep pull. On 23 April 1330, St George's Day, Henry VI of England landed at Calais in his kingdom of France. After remaining in Calais until July, the royal party moved on to Rouen, the capital of Normandy. Despite what had been positioned as a pressing need for Henry's French coronation, the English would linger at Rouen for 16 months. Bedford may have hoped to regain control of Reims, but Charles was proving too hard to dislodge from his

newly won positions. In November 1431, the procession finally left, heading not for Reims, but for Paris.

On 2 December, Henry arrived at Saint-Denis, the church that was the traditional mausoleum of the Kings of France. After two nights spent there in reflection, the nine-year-old entered Paris on 4 December, two days before his tenth birthday. The city put on a spectacular pageant to welcome the boy king. Three large heart-shaped displays poured forth white doves and flowers as he passed. The character of St Denis, the patron saint of France, featured throughout, but the arms of St George were also prominent. In one display, Henry was confronted by a large image of himself seated on a throne wearing two crowns. In his hands he held the royal coats of arms of England and France. Behind him stood the gathered councillors of both nations, ready to advise and support him. It was clear that this ceremony was an extension and continuation of the one in England. Henry was king of both realms by equal right. The idea that his English possession might take primacy was understandably underplayed in Paris. A new world order was being created.

The coronation took place at the Cathedral of Notre-Dame de Paris on 16 December 1431, ten days after Henry's tenth birthday. To the dismay of the Bishop of Paris, whose church it was, Cardinal Beaufort insisted on conducting the ceremony and crowning his great-nephew. A feast followed the service, as it had in London, though the citizens of Paris became almost immediately unsettled. They felt they had not been given the chance to provide produce for the feast nor to sell enough goods in the bustling city before the royal party prepared to leave. They had lavished a fortune on the reception of the English and were left out of pocket and disgruntled. Beating a hasty retreat, Henry was rushed back through Rouen and Calais, arriving at Dover on 29 January 1432.

Arriving in London on St Valentine's Day, 14 February 1431, Henry was treated to another display of pageantry. London Bridge was filled with scenes and figures, with the arms of both England and France prominent. At the drawbridge halfway along the bridge, Henry was met by figures representing Nature, Grace and Fortune. Further along, he encountered the figure of a king, surrounded by ladies representing the virtues, who presented him with a scroll that read, 'Honour of kings in every man's sight, Of common custom loves equity and right'. As he moved into the city, he saw a castle made of green jasper with a green tree on either side to represent his two kingdoms.

Henry was then greeted by figures of St Edward and St Louis, canonised kings of each nation, flanked by a line of all the kings of each realm up to Henry VI. Later, giant models representing the Holy Trinity welcomed the little king surrounded by angels who sang 'heavenly songs'. When Henry finally reached Westminster, he was allowed to rest, but the next day was required to receive the mayor and aldermen of London, who brought him gifts. Henry had undergone two coronation ceremonies, both of which were complex, intense and weighty, and he was barely ten years old. It must have been overwhelming and bewildering for such a young boy to be thrust to the forefront and represent so much expectation in such a small frame. The experiences of the previous two years would leave a permanent mark on the boy, helping to define the man he would become. That was part of the point of a coronation – to change a person. The question was whether it would be for the better or not.

The other tangled outcome of Henry's coronation in France was the permanent and indissoluble statement it made about the English Kingdom of France. Bedford's sole purpose was to preserve his brother's victories until his nephew was old enough to inherit them and make the most of them. In his mind, there was no going back, but at the very moment France was resurgent, and England was beginning to struggle, Bedford doubled down. A coronation could not be undone. Henry was, in the eyes of the law, of God and of about half of France, the rightful king. The issue was that Charles VII could claim the same thing. There was no room for compromise or negotiation. There could be only one King of France: Henry or Charles. Bedford's intention might have been to keep the stakes as high as that, but it left no room for anything to go wrong for England, at a time when things were beginning to slip.

The Trials of Joan of Arc

In the midst of Henry's French visit, matters did take a turn in the favour of the English. As Bedford waited for his nephew at

Calais, the city of Compiègne to the north of Paris declared for Charles VII despite lying in Burgundian territory. Duke Philip the Good demanded its surrender but was forced to send troops when the city refused. Charles hoped to bring the Burgundians back to his side, but Joan of Arc realised earlier than her king that there was no hope of doing so. She raised troops and marched to relieve Compiègne. On 23 May 1430, those within the city launched an offensive, joined by Joan's forces. The Burgundian commander was able to redeploy some of his men, and the Armagnacs decided to withdraw back to the city, despite Joan's incitements to them to fight on.

The rearguard was ordered to protect an orderly retreat, and Joan elected to remain with that portion of the army, riding her horse and displaying her banner. As the main part of the army entered Compiègne, the governor ordered the drawbridge raised and the gates closed. The rearguard was left trapped outside. It is unclear whether the governor acted to protect the city as Burgundians threatened to gain entry or to cut Joan off deliberately. There was a growing sense around Charles that Joan was no longer needed. He had done the hard part for them, and her

belligerent attitude and determination to push forward against the English was in opposition to the caution of many of Charles's advisers. There was also a growing sense that Joan held too much influence over the Armagnac faction. If she garnered credit for their success, it was at Charles's expense and that of the other men of his court. They were coming closer than any of them liked to taking military instructions from a woman. At Compiègne, they may have spotted the chance to be rid of her.

Surrounded by Burgundian forces who jeered and called for her surrender, Joan tried to fight until she was dragged from her horse and forced to give herself up. She was soon sold by her captors to their allies, the English, then at Rouen with the young King Henry. It was decided that Joan would stand trial for heresy. Allowing prophecy to be seen to be on the side of Charles VII was damaging to the English cause. If God was sending messages to Joan that would lead to Charles's coronation as the rightful King of France, it was clear whose side He was on. The English needed to change that perception, and the best way to do it was to discredit Joan's visions. If they were the work of the Devil, then Henry could still have right on his side. Joan, still aged just 19, was subjected to torture, deprived of sleep, and possibly threatened with rape in order to cause her to confess. Eventually, she told her tormentors that she had lied about the visions and voices she heard. She put on a dress instead of the military man's clothes she had previously worn. She was found guilty of heresy.

However, one conviction for heresy was not sufficient to incur the death penalty. A repentant heretic could only be put to death for a second incident of heresy. Unwilling to let the matter lie, the English pursued a second conviction. Joan soon recanted, withdrawing her confession of heresy. She may have done this as a matter of conscience, but it is also clear that her barbaric treatment continued. Threats of rape may have encouraged her to put back on her man's clothing to protect herself. Tired, frightened

and confused, Joan might have been duped and pushed into a second heresy trial. The result was a foregone conclusion.

Joan was led into the Vieux-Marché, the town square in Rouen, on 30 May 1431. She was tied to a tall wooden pillar as bundles of sticks were piled around her feet. A crucifix was held before the teenager as the pyre was set alight. Those gathered in the square watched her burn to death. At the end of the day, the remaining ashes were swept up and thrown into the River Seine to prevent their use as relics. In an effort to reclaim the moral high ground and damage the cause of their rival, the English had inflicted great cruelty on a young woman. Joan had believed to the end that Charles would come to save her, but he made no effort to do so. He would distance himself from Joan and her part in his victories for decades until an inquest in 1450 and a second one in 1452, followed by a retrial in 1456, found Joan innocent of the crime of heresy. Joan was made a saint in 1920 and became a patron saint of France in 1922, almost half a millennium after her success was repaid with suffering.

Joan's capture and trial may explain why Henry VI's party had lingered so long in Rouen before his coronation in Paris. Almost as soon as the young king was back in England, things began to unravel anew for the English Kingdom of France. John, Duke of Bedford was in his early forties when he saw his nephew off at the coast of Normandy. In 1423, he had married Anne of Burgundy, the sister of Duke Philip the Good. The couple had no children when Anne died in November 1432 as plague gripped Paris. Being single allowed John to make a strategic marriage alliance to bolster the English efforts in France further. He agreed with the ancient and powerful House of Luxembourg to marry Jacquetta of Luxembourg, the daughter of Peter, Count of St Pol. The 17-year-old bride was married to her middle-aged husband on 20 April 1433.

A Lost Ally

Philip, Duke of Burgundy was outraged. Not only had Bedford failed to observe the expected one year of mourning for Philip's sister, but he had also failed to consult the duke, England's chief ally, on such a critical matter. How genuine Philip's indignity was is unclear. He may have used the moment as an excuse to take a decision he wanted to make anyway. With no small diplomatic effort, the first peace talks between England and France since Troyes in 1420 took place at the Congress of Arras in August and September 1435. Neither king was present, but their representatives sought a way to establish peace. The problem for the English was their inflexibility after having Henry VI crowned King of France. For all the talking, there was no solution to that problem that avoided embarrassment and dishonour. The English delegation left with nothing settled before the Congress ended.

A more significant and immediate problem lay in the arrival of the Burgundian party, led by Duke Philip. Among his delegation was Louis, the new Count of St Pol and Jacquetta's brother. Their father had died within months of the match between her and Bedford. Philip submitted himself to King Charles VII, abandoning his 15-year alliance with England. Whether he was driven to this by his brother-in-law's remarriage or spotted a turning of the tide that he meant to ride is unclear. Charles VII denounced the murder of Duke Philip's father, John the Fearless. He swore to bring those guilty of the killing to justice, despite the fact that Charles was considered the driving force behind the assassination. Philip gained land in return and was personally exempted from giving homage to Charles for any of his lands, though it was agreed that the practice would resume after either man's death. For England, this visit to the table of peace negotiations had been a disaster.

Paris had been held thanks to the Burgundian alliance. Bedford was pushed back to Rouen in Normandy and, a week before the Congress of Arras ended on 21 September, John, Duke of Bedford died aged 46. He had maintained the astonishing successes of his brother Henry V for

LISTEN TO THE
PODCAST

The Burgundians

almost 15 years. Bedford was a gifted administrator and military commander. His reputation is tarnished by his role in the harsh treatment meted out to Joan of Arc, though he had ruthlessly seen off the greatest threat to the English position in France. John was buried at Rouen Cathedral. When Charles VII's son visited as King Louis XI, his men enthusiastically encouraged him to have Bedford's tomb torn down. Louis's reported response is a testament to the reputation Bedford held in France.

What honour shall it be to us, or to you, to break this monument and to pull out of the ground and take up the dead bones of him, whom in his life, neither my father nor your progenitors with all their power, puissance and friends were once able to make fly one foot backward, but by his strength, wit and policy, kept them all out of the principal dominions of the realm of France, and out of this noble and famous Duchy of Normandy: wherefore I say, first God have his soul, and let his body now lie in rest, which when alive, would have disquieted the proudest of us all: and as for the tombe, I assure you, it is not as decent, nor convenient for him, as his honour and acts deserved, although it were much richer and more beautiful.

The English Kingdom of France needed a new champion. The identity of that person was hotly debated in England, where factions increasingly divided the court of the teenage King Henry VI. Whoever it would be would face the daunting task of confronting the new alliance between Charles and Philip. The Armagnacs and Burgundians were moving closer to viewing themselves as a single French polity once more. As England's strength on the Continent wavered again, the impossibility of winning may have become clear, but inescapable too was the compulsion not to lose. The fall of continental territory invariably brought shockwaves across the Channel.

Perhaps the fact that Louis XI would come to stand in Rouen Cathedral to protect the tomb of John, Duke of Bedford is the greatest sign of what John had achieved and how precarious the English grip on France had become. One of the most controversial figures in 15th-century England was about to take his first steps on the international stage.

Chapter 11

The Rivals

The rivalry of Cardinal Beaufort and Humphrey, Duke of Gloucester :
Richard, Duke of York is sent to France : Henry VI begins the search
for peace with France : York returns to France : The fall of Humphrey,
Duke of Gloucester : Cade's Rebellion : The rivalry between York and
Somerset : The loss of the Hundred Years' War

I n England, the government had been continuing in the name of the young Henry VI. The day moved closer when he might be old enough to rule for himself, but in the meantime it remained fragile. Men had to be careful not to assume too much power and authority since their enemies might seek to use it against them and, one day, an adult king might resent it. But they were presented with an unprecedented opportunity to feather their own nests, and no one wanted to be the one left behind.

In the midst of this febrile and tense atmosphere, fractures were beginning to deepen and harden. Without a king to provide a lead, disputes lay unsettled and festering. The most explosive of the feuds was between two of the king's closest remaining male relatives. His uncle Humphrey, Duke of Gloucester became the last surviving son of Henry IV on Bedford's death. His brother Henry V had wanted him as regent, but he was deselected by the council, either because they mistrusted him or because they wanted a bigger share of power. Perhaps it was a bit of both.

Cardinal Henry Beaufort, Bishop of Winchester, was half-brother to Henry IV, uncle to Henry V and great-uncle to Henry VI. As a wealthy churchman, he had become the chief source of funding for a government perpetually in need of money for the war in France. With no children of his own, Cardinal Beaufort focussed his hopes on his nephews. The oldest living nephew was John, Earl of Somerset, who had been captured at the Battle of Baugé in 1421 and would remain a prisoner until 1438. John's younger brother, Edmund, was active in the wars in France too.

The choices in England were becoming increasingly stark: to pursue the war or find a way to make peace. Cardinal Beaufort favoured peace, perhaps because he was a man of God, perhaps because his vast trade interests were suffering during the war, particularly with the Burgundian alliance lost. Perhaps it was simply costing him a fortune he knew he would never recoup. Humphrey stood against this. He was utterly committed to pursuing his brothers' work in France following his experience at Agincourt.

He was 25 when he joined his brother's great stand for the Lancastrian crown in the mud of France. Fighting in the vanguard, Humphrey had been knocked down. As French knights loomed over him to deliver the killing blow, a figure in glinting armour stepped astride his prone body and drove the enemy back. That figure was Henry V, and his men dragged Humphrey to safety. Henry had come so close to the enemy that a blade sliced a piece from the crown on his helmet, but he had saved Humphrey's life. Completing his big brother's work was Humphrey's only way to repay that debt. Humphrey was also interested in books and art. His library forms the basis of the Bodleian Library in Oxford today, where visitors can still study in Duke Humfrey's Library.

By the 1430s, the feud between Cardinal Beaufort and Humphrey was out of control. When Bedford died, Humphrey became heir presumptive to his young nephew. The need for unity quelled the feud briefly, but by 1439 Gloucester was again complaining bitterly in Parliament about his uncle's actions, which defied Henry V's wishes. Humphrey may have been the obvious choice to go to France in his brother's place, but he had no intention of leaving London and surrendering the government to Cardinal Beaufort. Instead, he nominated a candidate for the post. Richard, 3rd Duke of York was born in September 1411. His father was Richard of Conisburgh, Earl of Cambridge, who had been executed for his role in the Southampton Plot in 1415. York's uncle, Edward, had died in the vanguard at Agincourt the same year and York had inherited his lands and titles. York's position was bolstered when his maternal uncle Edmund Mortimer, 5th Earl of March also died childless, so he also inherited his uncle's vast wealth and landholdings around the Welsh Marches. The problem was that he also acquired the Mortimer claim to the throne.

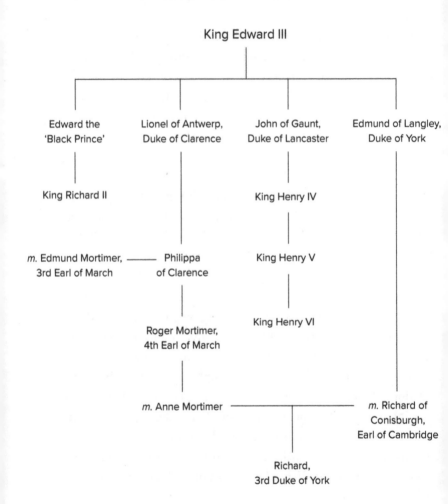

Cardinal Beaufort had his own preferred candidate for the role in France: his nephew Edmund Beaufort. In 1427, Edmund had become embroiled in a scandal around Henry V's widow, Catherine of Valois. There were stories that the two were engaged in an affair, which sent panic through the government. If the young queen remarried while the king was so young, his step-father might have the kind of influence they had sought to prevent Humphrey from holding. The council pushed through new legislation to try to stop a dowager queen from remarrying without the permission of the king. If she were to do so, her new husband would forfeit all of his goods and titles. If Catherine and Edmund had been falling in love, the new provision ended any talk of marriage. Catherine would find a way around this restriction, though.

Shortly after the new law was created, Catherine entered a relationship with a Welshman named Owen Tudor. Owen was a handsome young man the same age as the dowager queen. One story claims she saw him emerging from a pond after swimming, another that he was dancing in her presence and spun too much, falling into her lap. Whatever the truth, they became a couple, though there is some debate about whether they became legally married. The new law failed because Owen had no lands or titles to take away. The couple would have three sons, Edmund, Jasper and Edward Tudor. The older two half-brothers of the king would play central roles in later events.

The Lieutenant-General of France

It was eventually settled that York should become Lieutenant-General of France for a term of one year. His powers were drastically reduced from Bedford's regency authority, and his outlook could only be short-term. It is possible the appeal for the government of sending York lay in getting this Mortimer heir out of the kingdom. Perhaps they meant him to fail in France. In the same month that York was appointed, Edmund Beaufort was given command of a new expeditionary force funded by his uncle, the cardinal. By the time the new men arrived in France, Paris had fallen to Charles VII. York based his government in Rouen, and his military support was provided by John Talbot.

York's year in France was reasonably successful. Some towns were retaken, though several larger ones, like Harfleur, remained in French hands. He extended the policy of demolishing any castle that was taken which was not strategically vital. He demonstrated an even hand in government at a time when the Normans could have been looking for a way out of ongoing taxation and war. At the end of his term, York made it known he wished to return home. His wages were unpaid, and he was being forced to fund the government of the English Kingdom of France from his own substantial pocket. Perhaps that was the idea. York was replaced by Richard Beauchamp, 13th Earl of Warwick, who had been the young Henry VI's guardian and tutor. In 1437, at 16, Henry was declared to have reached the age of majority. Freed from one role, Warwick, then aged 55, accepted a new challenge in France.

In England, Henry VI wrote to his sheriffs on 4 December 1437, two days before his sixteenth birthday, instructing them to restore order in the country. He complained that 'misgoverned men' committed 'great robberies, ravishment of women, burning of houses, manslaughters and many other great riots and inconveniences'. The king enclosed with each letter a copy of Edward I's Statute of Winchester of 1285, which remained the basis for local law and order until the 19th century. Henry also turned his attention to the war overseas, discontent with which was fuelling unrest at home. His response was what some hoped for but not what others expected.

Henry VI appointed ambassadors to visit Charles VII and

begin negotiating peace. As a sign of goodwill, he announced the release of the Duke of Orleans, who had been an English prisoner since Agincourt in 1415. Orleans finally returned to France in 1440, 25 years after his capture. The aim was to break the political stalemate in the aftermath of the Treaty of Arras that had seen Burgundy rejoin the King of France. If there was a more sinister scheme, it was that Orleans was a member of the line of succession and might destabilise France. Even if that was part of the plan, it did nothing to calm Humphrey. Henry V had left explicit instructions in his will that Orleans was not to be released, and Humphrey disapproved loudly of the decision. In 1438, Cardinal Beaufort had negotiated the return of his nephew, John Beaufort, Earl of Somerset in return for the Count of Eu, another Agincourt prisoner Henry V had expressly instructed should not be released.

When Warwick died at Rouen in April 1439, it sent English plans in France into turmoil and set Cardinal Beaufort and Humphrey at one another's throats again. Gloucester considered

taking up the post himself but remained wary of leaving England and of the cardinal's opposition to such an appointment. Cardinal Beaufort quickly installed his two nephews, John and Edmund Beaufort, among five military men in temporary control of English lands. His intention was that John should become the heir to Bedford in France. Gloucester once again thrust his own candidate, York, into the mix.

On 2 July 1440, York was appointed Lieutenant-General of France again, this time for five years and with greatly increased powers that came close to Bedford's regency authority. His salary was two and a half times the previous level, some paid before he left. After leading an army to support Talbot at Pontoise, York settled in at Rouen. In England, the vicious power politics took a new turn. Humphrey's second wife was Eleanor Cobham, a woman of lowly origins whom Humphrey seems to have genuinely loved. They shared many interests in learning, art and culture and maintained a lavish court. On 21 October 1441, Eleanor was found guilty of witchcraft.

It was alleged that she had engaged astrologers to predict the death of Henry VI, which would make her husband king. Eleanor admitted purchasing fertility medicine from Margery Jourdemayne, the Witch of Eye, in order to try to conceive a child, but denied any treasonous necromancy. Eleanor escaped the death penalty because it turned out there was no legal mechanism to try a noblewoman. No one had ever thought about it. The law was changed so that women could be tried by a panel of their (male) peers, just as noblemen were. Eleanor was forced to walk in public penance in the streets of London, her marriage was annulled and she was placed into custody for the rest of her life. Accusations of witchcraft against

LISTEN TO THE
PODCAST

The Rise of the
Beauforts

prominent women were increasingly common in the 15th century. It was almost certainly a political attack. Henry V had imprisoned his stepmother for it in order to seize her lands. In Eleanor's case, the real target was Humphrey, who was forced to retire from public life.

The Search for Peace

With his belligerent uncle out of the way, Henry VI pressed on with trying to negotiate a peaceful end to the war. Charles VII, smelling blood in the water, consistently refused to participate. In 1443, the king agreed to allow his cousin John Beaufort to lead a fresh army into France. He was to do this outside of York's control and in pursuit of lands and titles that had belonged to Bedford and which, if recovered, he could keep. In addition, Somerset was raised to the rank of duke, the highest tier of nobility, an honour usually reserved as a reward for extremely good service. Somerset instead received it in anticipation of any achievements. Cardinal Beaufort's plans were progressing smoothly.

Somerset landed at Cherbourg in August 1443 and pressed south into Maine and Anjou. Here he joined up with his brother Edmund, now Earl of Dorset. Immediately, they turned round and marched back north. After weeks of laying an unsuccessful siege at Pouancé, they moved on to La Guerche. The town fell quickly, and Somerset's men ran amok. The Duke of Brittany, in whose lands the town stood, was forced to pay for its return and compelled to sign a truce. It might have been a victory, except that the Duke of Brittany was an ally of England. His brother was at Henry's court and made furious representations to the king. Henry denied any knowledge of Somerset's actions and showered money and gifts on the irate envoy. When the king wrote a formal letter of censure to Somerset, ordering him to make reparations

NOBLE RANKS

Duke or Duchess: The highest noble rank in England, beneath a king or prince, was a duke. The title was first introduced to England by Edward III in 1337 for his oldest son, the Black Prince. The first person outside the royal family to receive the title was William de la Pole, who became Duke of Suffolk in 1448.

Marquess or Marchioness: A relatively uncommon title, it sat just below a duke in precedence. The title had parallels in Norman France, the Marchio, and in Germany, the Margrave. Robert de Vere, Earl of Oxford was the first in England to receive this promotion as Marquess of Oxford.

Earl or Countess: Derived from the Anglo-Saxon ealdorman who administered the shires; they became earls under King Cnut. Following the Norman Conquest, the title became hereditary.

Viscount or Viscountess: The root of this title may lie in the Holy Roman Empire, where a vice-comes was the deputy of a count. It was first introduced in England under Henry VI, who gave the title to Viscount Beaumont in England and in France.

Baron or Baroness: The lowest rank of nobility. A baron held land from the king without any higher title.

and never to repeat his actions again, the strength of feeling was such that even Cardinal Beaufort added his name to the list of vexed signatories.

After returning to England in disgrace, Somerset died on 27 May 1444, four days before the first birthday of his only legitimate child, Lady Margaret Beaufort. There were suggestions that he had taken his own life as a result of his shame. Before the expedition, Somerset had been ill, and the king had written to enquire when he would be well enough to travel. It is possible his misjudgement in France had been a result of the same illness and that this claimed his life on his return. Edmund Beaufort became Earl of Somerset as his brother's heir, though he did not acquire the dukedom. Whether this unpleasant episode lay at the core of the emerging problems or was simply an extension of the ongoing factional tensions, York and Somerset were becoming bitter rivals. The feud between Cardinal Beaufort and Humphrey had found a home in the next generation.

Henry VI was relying increasingly on William de la Pole, Earl of Suffolk. He had been prominent in the war in France, and his family had lost a great deal there. Confronted by a king who had no interest in that fight, William adjusted his outlook and became something of a father figure to Henry. Aged 47 in 1444, William was tasked with negotiating a marriage for Henry that would smooth the peace negotiations. The earl knew it was a poisoned chalice and pleaded to be excused from the task, but Henry elevated him to the rank of marquis and dispatched him to France. Having hoped to marry a daughter of Charles VII, the French king demonstrated that he had no intention of repeating what his father had done. Instead, Henry was offered a niece of Charles's wife. Margaret of Anjou was the 14-year-old daughter of René, Duke of Anjou.

René maintained flimsy paper claims to the Crowns of Naples, Sicily, Aragon and Jerusalem, and had bankrupted the family in desperate bids to make one of them a reality. The thought of his daughter becoming Queen of England appealed to

LISTEN TO THE
PODCAST

Margaret Beaufort

the duke. His penniless state meant that he had no dowry to offer for his daughter. Undaunted, Henry agreed not only to accept no dowry but also to hand land in France back to René and Charles VII in return for agreeing to the match. In his desperation for peace, Henry had played the vital hand of a king's marriage to no certain advantage. He knew it would prove unpopular in England, or was told so, because he kept the arrangement a secret for as long as possible. Margaret arrived in England in April 1445, and the couple were married. When it came to light, there was uproar.

York returned to England at Christmas 1445 as his commission in France ended. He appeared to expect to be reappointed but, in Parliament, he found he was forced to defend himself from accusations of mismanagement. Henry had, unbeknownst to most, agreed to hand over chunks of land to Charles by the end of April 1446. After delaying decisions for as long as he could, Henry finally appointed a Lieutenant-General of France on 24 December 1446. It was not York but Somerset who received the honour. A new deadline to hand over the territory in France was set for April 1447, with a warning it would not be moved again. Parliament was summoned to sit in February 1447 in Cambridge. At the last moment the location was changed to Bury St Edmunds, in the heartlands of William de la Pole, Marquis of Suffolk.

Loyal Opposition?

As Humphrey arrived in the town for the session of Parliament, he was informed that he was to remain in his lodgings and make no effort to see his nephew, the king. A few days later a group of noblemen, including Edmund Beaufort, now Marquis of Somerset, informed Humphrey that he was under arrest

for treason. He had, they explained, been exposed, plotting to murder his nephew and steal the Crown. Humphrey was put into a cell, and within days he was dead. The official cause of his death was a stroke brought on by the shock, but rumours of murder, probably poisoning, sprang up immediately. Humphrey, Duke of Gloucester, the last son of Henry IV, died on 23 February 1447, aged 56. He was buried at St Albans Abbey. If Cardinal Beaufort felt he had won a victory, it was short-lived. He died, as the last child of John of Gaunt, aged 71 on 11 April, six weeks after the nephew who had been his political rival.

With his uncle gone, Henry handed the county of Maine over to Charles VII. The timing suggests that Humphrey had been viewed as a blockage, which had now been removed. His uncle's death created a fresh problem for Henry, though. Humphrey had widespread popular support for his aggressive stance against France. He had been heir to Henry VI for as long as he remained childless. Those two problematic positions needed a new home. The answer was obvious. Whether he had liked it or not, York had been consistently named by Humphrey as among those unjustly excluded from government as he was, and he was always top of Humphrey's list. Popular support for war in France slid to the man who had been relatively successful there as governor. York was viewed as heir presumptive to Henry now, too, as his senior male relative of the blood royal. Layered on top of this was the tricky question of York's Mortimer heritage. Henry had rid himself of one problem but might have created an even bigger one. For the first time, loyal opposition to the House of Lancaster had its home outside the House of Lancaster.

In December 1447, York was appointed Lord Lieutenant of Ireland for ten years. The office was the most prestigious one available after France, and York's Mortimer connections made him a significant landowner and magnate there. York took the post willingly, declining to appoint a deputy and deciding to go to Ireland himself. Perhaps he hoped distance would ease Henry's mind. Most of Ireland had always been beyond the control of the English Crown, even if they claimed otherwise. The area around Dublin was generally loyal. York was the Earl of Ulster, so had some control in the north, but outside that area the Irish lords felt relatively free. York's time in Ireland, like his time in France, would prove successful, if unspectacular.

In France, Somerset was proving a fractious character. He had won the prize his uncle had wanted for him at a time when it was undoubtedly a poisoned chalice. Charles VII had been patiently building his arsenal of new gunpowder weapons to counter English tactics on the battlefield. Pointed stakes might stop horses, but not cannonballs. Henry VI had displayed his all-consuming desire for peace. The time was right to strike. All Charles needed was a casus belli – a cause for war. When Somerset repeatedly wrote to the King of France in derogatory terms, Charles complained it was not the respect he was due or the cordial relationship he had enjoyed with York. At one point, French messengers refused to deliver Somerset's words to their master.

In 1449, skirmishes broke out along the Norman border as Charles probed the defences. In March an English force seized the town of Fougères, and in July, Charles declared war on England. On 26 August 1449, a French army poured into the duchy. Somerset surrendered Rouen on 29 October and withdrew to Caen, a city that belonged to the Duke of York. On 1 July 1450, when a cannonball landed between his wife and children, Somerset gave up York's town and fled to England. Normandy was lost again. Unbeknownst to anyone in 1450, this was its final loss to England.

At home, things were going from bad to worse. The military failures, the arrival of those ejected from homes in France, and unpaid, frustrated soldiers loitering around the south coast were a recipe for trouble. William de la Pole, now Duke of Suffolk, was hauled before Parliament and blamed for all the kingdom's woes. He protested, but the House of Commons in particular was in no mood to compromise. Henry stepped in to stop the proceedings against his favourite. He found Suffolk guilty of some minor financial irregularities and banished him from England for five years. The move was meant to protect Suffolk, but, as his ship sailed on 1 May 1450, he was intercepted, dragged into a small boat and beheaded. His body was dumped on Dover beach with his head on a spike beside it. Some were keen to see York's hand, from Ireland, at work in the murder.

By June, the rebels had coalesced behind a leader named Jack Cade and gathered at Blackheath. The parallels with the Peasants' Revolt 70 years earlier were plain and startling. The group issued a document entitled The Complaint of the Poor Commons of Kent, which bemoaned the state of the government and the country. Henry was uncharacteristically aggressive, gathering an army and moving towards Blackheath.

When he found the open space deserted, he sent a small force to pursue the peasants. The withdrawal had been a feint. An ambush led to fierce fighting, on 18 June, in the forests of the Weald of Kent. Both the leaders, Humphrey and William Stafford, were killed and their armour was stolen by the rebels. These former soldiers were not the rabble the king had expected. Henry fled the capital to sanctuary in the Midlands. The violence spread as, on 28 June, the Bishop of Salisbury was murdered after giving a service at one of his churches. He was dragged to the top of a nearby hill and beaten to death, with the mob taking scraps of his bloodied clothes as grisly trophies. His main offence seemed to have been officiating at the king's unpopular marriage.

Cade returned to Blackheath to find the royal forces gone. He moved up to Southwark on the south bank of the Thames and, from there, crossed London Bridge on 3 July. His men cut the ropes on the drawbridge as they went so it could not be closed

on them, but many Londoners welcomed the rebels. As in 1381, many within the capital shared the same concerns and complaints as those rebelling. As he entered the capital, Cade reportedly struck the London Stone with his dagger. The stone stood on the south side of Candlewick Street, which is now Cannon Street, and was moved to the north side in 1742 to make way for increasing traffic. The stone's origin is unknown, but by the medieval period it was considered ancient. Its original purpose is similarly unclear. One suggestion is that it may have been placed there by the Romans as a point from which they measured all distances in Britain.

The meaning of striking the stone is similarly lost, but the meaning of what Cade was reported as shouting was clear. 'Now is Mortimer lord of this city!' Cade began to use the name John Mortimer, and claimed to be a member of that family. The allusion to their claim to the throne in a failing kingdom was obvious and deeply threatening. Many thoughts turned to York immediately. Henry's suspicion had led to his uncle's death. It had then fallen on York, a sentiment Henry's wife Margaret shared. The question on everyone's lips was whether York was driving events to position himself as an alternative king or whether Henry was seeing plots that were not there. If the latter, his reaction could create the very problems he feared by driving York and his support into opposition.

Cade's force held London for several days. They executed several men, including the Treasurer, an office targeted in 1381. The Tower of London held out under Lord Scales, a veteran of France. As discipline slipped among the rebels, Scales led a force out of the Tower to retake the city. Each evening, the rebels had left London to return to Southwark. On 5 July, Scales

LISTEN TO THE
PODCAST

Cade's Rebellion

waited for them to cross and then set about repairing the draw-bridge. Upon hearing this, the rebels flooded back to the bridge. Fighting broke out at about nine o'clock and lasted all night. Bodies fell into the dark Thames, to be dragged away by the tide as the bridge caught fire and blazed in the night sky. Eventually, the fire forced them apart.

In the morning, the Archbishop of York rode out to the bedraggled rebels and offered them a pardon if they returned home. They accepted and left. Almost immediately, Cade's pardon was withdrawn, on the basis that he had taken it in the name of John Mortimer when he was really Jack Cade. He was not the only one pursued. Henry sent men into Kent to exact a heavy revenge. The inquisitions that followed Cade's Rebellion became known as the Harvest of Heads. The Mortimer name had shaken the king. On hearing of the uprising, York returned from Ireland, stating his intention to help the king. Henry ordered his cousin arrested as soon as he landed in Wales. York evaded the trap and gathered men from the Mortimer lands in the Welsh Marches as he moved toward London, writing to Henry at each stop to reassure him he meant only to help. This moment set the tone for a decade of collapsing relationships that would drag England into civil war.

The Road to Dartford

In May 1451, Parliament heard that King Henry's debts stood at £372,000 (equivalent to around £232 million today). Henry's household cost £24,000 a year to run, and his income was £5,000. The maths simply did not add up. The king gave away land and offices far too freely. On one occasion, he granted the same post to two men on the same day simply because they both asked for it in turn. Suppliers refused to deliver food to the royal kitchens because they knew they would not be paid.

The session of Parliament was closed by Henry, who was furious after one member of the House of Commons with links to York suggested Parliament should recognise York as heir to the child-less Henry. The MP, Thomas Young, was thrown into the Tower for 'things said by him in the House of Commons', though he later received compensation for breach of his right to free speech within Parliament.

When violence erupted between the Earl of Devon and Lord Bonville in the West Country, only York moved to bring it to an end, forcing both men to cease their fighting. In London, Somerset had returned in 1450 and slipped into the space at Henry's side left by Suffolk. Despite York's successes and Somerset's failures, Henry preferred the company and advice of his Beaufort relative. By early 1452, York had grown frustrated by his exclusion from government. He wrote to towns along the Marches complaining that 'derogation, loss of merchandise, lesion of honour, and villainy, is said and reported generally unto the English nation' as a result of the loss of France. He openly blamed Somerset for that loss and for whispering in the king's ear to turn Henry against him.

York raised a force that one report states consisted of 3,000 gunners and 8,000 men-at-arms under him, 6,000 men under the Earl of Devon and 6,000 under Lord Cobham, with seven ships on the Thames 'with their stuff'. York sought to impose himself on Henry, demanding what he considered his rightful place at the top table of government. Henry sent a delegation to ask York for his demands. He asked only that Somerset be arrested and put on trial for treason. Henry agreed. York disbanded his force and went to the king. As he entered the king's presence, York was shocked to be confronted

LISTEN TO THE
PODCAST

The Origins of the
Wars of the Roses

by Somerset, free and standing at the king's side. York was placed under arrest and led back to London as a prisoner. Forced to swear an embarrassing oath in front of a crowd at St Paul's Cathedral never to raise an army against Henry again, he was only released when a rumour reached London that York's ten-year-old son Edward, Earl of March was raising a force to free his father.

In 1453, buoyed by his victory over York, Henry was revitalised. He sent a fresh army into France in defiance of his peace policy. The force was led by John Talbot, who had been created Earl of Shrewsbury in 1442 and was now in his mid-sixties. Talbot landed with 3,000 men near Bordeaux, which had been captured by the French. He was reinforced by 3,000 more led by his fourth son John, Viscount Lisle. As they marched to meet a French force, Talbot outstripped most of the army, arriving with only 500 men-at-arms and 800 archers who had managed to keep up. They found a French garrison stationed at a priory and quickly drove them away. Encouraged by news that the French were retreating, Talbot gave chase. He rode his small force into an army that was not retreating. Despite realising the odds stacked against him, Talbot refused to pull back as the rest of his forces engaged.

The French position was well secured, and the English attacks floundered. Still, Old Talbot would not withdraw, perhaps reminded of his own charges laid against Sir John Fastolf. There was bitter fighting, but the English were hopelessly outnumbered as French cannon ripped through them. It was almost a reversal of the Battle of Crecy. Talbot was killed, as was his son, along with up to 4,000 English soldiers. The finest, most experienced and respected general at the disposal of the English Crown had thrown himself recklessly into the fray

LISTEN TO THE
PODCAST

The Hundred
Years' War

and been lost. The French built a monument to him where he fell. Bordeaux and the rest of Gascony quickly fell to the French.

The war in France reached an end on 17 July 1453. The Battle of Castillon is generally considered the end of the Hundred Years' War. For all the English focus on battles like Crecy, Poitier and Agincourt, the bottom line was that England lost the war. The town of Calais and the region of Gascony, the reduced remnant

COLLAPSE AFTER
CASTILLON

ENGLAND

FLANDERS

• ROUEN

• RHEIMS

• PARIS

KINGDOM
OF FRANCE

BURGUNDY

• LIMOGES

• BORDEAUX

VENAISSIN

TOULOUSE
•

of Aquitaine, were the last pieces of territory held by the English Crown.

When news reached England of the disastrous defeat, the loss of Talbot, of Gascony, and of the war, Henry was at the royal hunting lodge at Clarendon in Wiltshire. He had chosen to ignore a serious feud erupting into violence between the Percy family and their local rivals, the Neville family in the northeast of England. Instead, he was heading to try to resolve a dispute in the south of Wales. The argument was over the inheritance of Cardiff Castle. It was held by Richard Neville, Earl of Warwick, in right of his wife, but the husband of her half-sister laid claim to it too. That husband was Edmund Beaufort, Duke of Somerset. Henry had found in favour of Somerset, but Warwick had no intention of giving the castle up. Henry was travelling west to force Warwick to surrender to Somerset.

Whether the news from Castillon reached Henry is unclear. He had been unusually driven and active over the last year or more, and it appeared to have taken a toll. Henry's grandfather was Charles VI of France, who suffered severe bouts of mental illness. It now appeared that Henry might have inherited something similar. The stress seemed to show on him suddenly. In August 1453, at the age of 31, Henry suffered a complete mental and physical collapse. He became catatonic and unable to move or feed himself. Everything was sent into a spiral. The person of the king was still central to the functioning of the government. No one knew how long this episode might last or if the king would ever recover. With Henry oblivious, England faced a new problem and looked for old solutions. The catastrophes of the reign of Henry VI had only just begun.

Wars of the Roses.

Chapter 12

The Wars of the Roses

Henry VI falls ill : York is appointed Protector : The First Battle of
St Albans : York is made Protector again : The Yorkist lords are
forced into exile : York claims the throne : York is killed at the Battle
of Wakefield : His son becomes King Edward IV : Henry VI returns to
the throne briefly : The Battles of Barnet and Tewkesbury : The death
of Henry VI : George, Duke of Clarence is executed : Richard, Duke
of Gloucester's Scottish campaign : The Death of Edward IV :
The accession of Richard III : The Battle of Bosworth

The council and those closest to the king hid his debilitating illness for as long as possible. Nothing significant could be undertaken without the king's approval. England coasted along. As some wondered how long it would last, others questioned when, or if, the king might recover. The government was crippled, but most, like Henry, were oblivious to the threats this caused as the king's incapacity remained a secret. When Queen Margaret gave birth to her first child on 13 October 1453, he was named Edward and presented to the king. Henry offered no acknowledgement. His acceptance of his son was critical to the boy's legitimacy. Still, the king's illness was kept secret.

The ongoing problem had been hidden for more than six months before the moment of crisis all had dreaded arrived. On 22 March 1454, the Archbishop of Canterbury died. Royal involvement in appointing a new archbishop would be expected, and it was too big a decision to be taken informally without the king's knowledge. The question was how to provide for long-term government in the effective absence of the king. Margaret laid claim to regency powers. One witness recorded that 'she desired to have the whole rule of this land'. Margaret wished to be allowed to appoint the great officers of state, control the Great Seal, appoint bishops and be provided with a sufficient income. Given royal debts, the last demand might have seemed tone-deaf.

In France, Margaret would have been expected to hold regency powers for her ill or absent husband. It was the accepted process there. But Margaret was not in France. England's nobility would still not accept female rule. It was not helpful that Margaret was not popular either: she was French and her marriage had cost England territory. The nobility recoiled at the queen's request, and scrambled to find an alternative answer. Margaret was deeply suspicious of York, sharing her husband's fear of his intentions. Just as Henry had driven York toward the edge of a precipice that forced him to push back, Margaret's demand for power backfired.

One final effort was made to reach the king. A delegation from Parliament was sent to Windsor to seek any sign of awareness in him, but found only his vacant eyes. With their return, Parliament resolved to act. York had been recalled to the council in November when the Duke of Norfolk, almost certainly at York's prompting, had laid charges of treason against Somerset, who had been in the Tower since then. On 27 March 1454, York accepted the office of Protector and Defender of the Realm and Church. Despite his poor relationship with Henry, his position as the most senior royal adult made him preferable to the queen. York was a safe option since he had experience and appeared ultimately loyal to the king, having never pressed his own claim to the throne. In searching for a way to proceed, Parliament fell back on the arrangements for Henry's minority when he had also been unable to rule. Thomas Bourchier, a grandson of Edward III and half-brother of the Duke of Buckingham, was made Archbishop of Canterbury. The new Lord Chancellor was Richard Neville, Earl of Salisbury, York's brother-in-law. Salisbury was Warwick's father, and the dispute over Cardiff Castle had pushed the powerful northern Neville family into York's camp.

York's government was even-handed. It included the king's half-brothers, Edmund and Jasper Tudor, and York oversaw the creation of little Edward as Prince of Wales in an effort to allay any fears about his own ambitions. In November, new ordinances were set out for the structure of a reformed royal household. The size and spiralling costs were to be returned to the levels they had been during the reign of the king's father, Henry V. It seemed like sensible efforts to address a financial disaster, but Queen Margaret viewed it as an attack on her position by York. Nevertheless, as

1454 progressed, England seemed to be moving onto an even keel. Then, Christmas came.

Recovery and Loss

On 25 December 1454, Henry VI stirred from almost 18 months of catatonia. Contemporaries saw a miracle. Later commentators have suggested that, if Henry's collapse was a disaster, then his recovery was a tragedy. As soon as the king was well enough, he was introduced to his son, of whom he said he had no memory. York was quickly dismissed from his post as Protector, and Salisbury was sacked as Chancellor. Somerset was freed from the Tower. It was a complete reversal, but now the royal court was even more suspicious of York. He had had a taste of power. What if he liked it? More worryingly, he had done a good job. What if the people liked it? York and Salisbury retreated into the north.

As summer approached in 1455, a Great Council was summoned to sit in the Midlands. York, Salisbury and Warwick were invited. They were nervous. Eight years earlier, Humphrey, Duke of Gloucester had been lured into Suffolk's heartlands and had not made it out alive. Now, they were being called into Henry's Lancastrian power base. What fate might await them there? The Yorkist lords gathered an army and marched south, aiming to intercept Henry before he reached the East Midlands. Each day, they wrote to the king to tell him where they were to explain that they were coming to prove their loyalty.

York found the king at St Albans, just north of London. The royal force was within the town walls as the Yorkists camped outside. On the morning of 22 May 1455, York arrayed his forces in Key Fields outside the gates in direct defiance of the oath he had given in 1452 never to put an army into the field again. A parlay ensued. It was traditional for armies to negotiate before a

YORK'S KEY ALLIES

Thomas Courtenay, Earl of Devon: Courtenay was an early ally of York. He was engaged in a long-running feud in the West Country with his neighbours the Bonville family. Courtenay was with York at Dartford in 1452. He would die in 1458 while travelling to London to attend the Loveday.

Richard Neville, Earl of Salisbury: Salisbury was the oldest son of Ralph Neville, Earl of Westmorland's second marriage, to Joan Beaufort, daughter of John of Gaunt. Salisbury acquired his title by marrying Alice Montagu, Countess of Salisbury. Holding a title in this was known as *de jure uxoris* – in right of his wife. The Neville family were initially loyal to Henry but transferred to York in 1453 after increasing disputes with royal favourites.

Richard Neville, Earl of Warwick: Salisbury's oldest son, Warwick continued the Neville family's rise in power. He married Anne Beauchamp, Countess of Warwick and became one of the most powerful men in the realm under Yorkist kingship. He would cause problems for his cousin, Edward IV, and become known as the Kingmaker.

battle. The Church viewed war between Christians as sinful, so it was the job of both leaders to try to defuse the situation and avoid the shedding of Christian blood. York demanded that Somerset be handed over to him. He would not be tricked again as he had been at Dartford. The reply from the king ordered everyone to disperse, or 'I shall destroy them every mother's son, and they be hanged, and drawn, and quartered that may be taken afterwards'.

Talks continued until around 11 o'clock, when it became clear no resolution would be found. York's men began an assault on the gates, defended by Lord Clifford. Warwick took his force around the walls to look for a weak spot and managed to break into some gardens. As they flooded through the narrow streets of St Albans, his men blew trumpets and shouted their war cry, 'À Warwick! À Warwick!' Those within the walls were caught unawares. They had not put their armour on as Warwick's archers loosed arrows into the marketplace. As chaos erupted, those on the barricades ran to find the source of the commotion, allowing York and Salisbury to break through the gates. The First Battle of St Albans was odd, taking place within the cramped street of a town instead of an open field, but it was a complete victory for York that gave him control of the government.

Somerset was killed as running fights spread through the streets. The Earl of Northumberland, the Percy rival of the Neville lords, also fell in what looked like a manhunt. Scores were being

settled in blood. Lord Clifford fell. The Duke of Buckingham was wounded by an arrow in the face. Somerset's son Henry Beaufort was so badly injured he had to be taken away on a cart. Even the king was struck in the neck by an arrow, and taken to a tanner's shop for treatment. With the battle won, York burst into the small room and confronted the king. If, as Henry and Margaret feared, York wanted the Crown, here was a chance to take it. If Henry died of the accidental wound, who would know that York had widened it? Instead, the duke fell to his knee, swore fealty to Henry, and took the king to the abbey for better treatment.

This battle is usually considered the beginning of the civil conflict known as the Wars of the Roses. Henry was escorted to London and ceremonially recrowned. When Parliament met, York was reinstated as Protector, though there was little evidence this time that Henry was ill. When York introduced an Act of Resumption, which would take back royal grants in order to balance the king's finances, Henry was suddenly recalled, and York was once more thrown out. Those in Parliament were the very people who had benefited from Henry's open-handed generosity. They had no intention of handing it all back. York returned to the political wilderness.

The Loveday

A stalemate set in. When Parliament gathered in March 1458, Henry attempted to resolve the tensions. York arrived with 400 men, Salisbury with 500 and Warwick with 600. The sons of Lancastrians killed at St Albans were baying for vengeance. Henry Beaufort was now Duke of Somerset and close to the king and queen, as his father had been. The new Earl of Northumberland, another Henry Percy, and the new Lord Clifford of Skipton joined him in his hatred of the Yorkist lords. These young lords were refused lodgings within London 'because they had come against the peace' with larger forces than the Yorkists.

The king led intense negotiations. The outcome was that the Yorkist lords should take full responsibility for the deaths at St Albans. They were required to pay reparations to the families of Somerset, Northumberland and Lord Clifford and fund a chantry chapel to say prayers for their souls. The Yorkists agreed, clearly seeking to end the ongoing trouble. Henry was delighted and ordered a Loveday to be held. He jubilantly paraded through London, followed by two columns of the royal faction and Yorkists, each holding hands with an enemy. It was a novel moment that was also awkward. York held Queen Margaret's hand. Salisbury, that of Somerset. Other than Henry, few in London could have believed it was over.

HENRY'S KEY ALLIES

Dukes of Somerset: The Beaufort family were cousins of Henry VI. Edmund Beaufort, 2nd Duke of York was a personal rival to Richard, Duke of York. Their relationship fed into the beginning of the Wars of the Roses. Edmund was killed in 1455 at the First Battle of St Albans and was succeeded by his son, Henry, 3rd Duke of Somerset. Henry led royal forces to victory at the Battles of Wakefield and Second St Albans. He was executed after the Battle of Hexham in 1464. He was succeeded by his younger brother Edmund, 4th Duke of Somerset, who remained loyal to Henry VI until Edmund was executed after the Battle of Tewkesbury in 1471.

Earls of Northumberland: The Percy family were rivals to the Neville family in the north of England. As the Neville family gravitated towards York, the Percy family grew closer to Henry VI. Henry, 2nd Earl was killed at the First Battle of St Albans. His son Henry, 3rd Earl died at the Battle of Towton in 1461. His son, another Henry, 4th Earl was eventually reconciled with Edward IV and led Richard III's rearguard at Bosworth. He was murdered during a tax revolt in 1489 amidst claims he had abandoned Richard III at Bosworth, leading to the king's death.

Lords Clifford: Thomas, Lord Clifford of Skipton died fighting for Henry VI at the First Battle of St Albans. His son, John, was among those who sought revenge on the Yorkist lords. John died fighting at Towton, after which his five-year-old son Henry vanished, only reappearing in 1485 to request the return of his family's property at Henry VII's first Parliament.

Humphrey Stafford, 1st Duke of Buckingham: Buckingham had served in France as a commander and remained loyal to Henry VI. He was injured at the First Battle of St Albans and killed at the Battle of Northampton in 1461. His grandson, Henry Stafford, 2nd Duke of Buckingham, was briefly close to Richard III before being executed for leading a rebellion in late 1483.

As Parliament disbanded, everyone returned to their lands, not to relax but to gather their forces. One chronicler was clear about the roots of the tension. 'The queen with such as were of her affinity ruled the realm as she liked, gathering riches innumerable.' Her new Treasurer, the Earl of Wiltshire, 'peeled the poor people'. As summer ended, York decided to act. He summoned Salisbury and Warwick to his fortress at Ludlow. As Salisbury marched south from Yorkshire, he encountered an army raised by Queen Margaret, commanded by Lord Audley, in Staffordshire. At the Battle of Blore Heath on 23 September, Salisbury used all of his military experience gained in France to confront the larger force.

Lined up on either side of a brook outside the range of each other's longbows, Salisbury's forces suddenly fled. Lord Audley charged, but the withdrawal was a trick. As soon as the royal forces were in the stream, Salisbury's turned and attacked. The royal army was overwhelmed, and Lord Audley killed. Aware of another force somewhere nearby, Salisbury hurried on to Ludlow. He paid a local friar to stand and fire a cannon through the evening and night to disorientate any pursuing army. When he arrived at Ludlow, he was joined by his oldest son Warwick, Captain of Calais, and a swelling number of York's men.

By the early days of October, York was ready. With the queen in the Midlands, he headed south and east towards London, aiming to repeat his effort to impose himself on Henry at Dartford in 1452. They had reached Worcester when news arrived that a royal army double the size of theirs was approaching. Henry himself was at the head, wearing his armour and flying royal banners. There would be no question that confronting this army would be an act of treason. The Yorkist lords swore oaths of allegiance to the king at Worcester Cathedral to demonstrate their loyalty, and marched back to Ludlow. Henry followed them.

At Ludlow, York ordered defensive earthworks dug as the royal army drew closer. On the night of 12 October, the two armies pitched camp. Henry offered a pardon to anyone who abandoned the Yorkist cause. In the night, the Calais garrison brought by Warwick scaled the earthworks and fled to the king. On learning the news that they had gone, taking details of the Yorkist defences and plans, the lords retired to Ludlow Castle for a council of war. In the morning, they were gone. York took his second son,

Edmund, to Ireland, and his oldest son Edward went with his uncle Salisbury and cousin Warwick to the south coast and then to Calais. Ludlow was sacked by the royal army. Soldiers looted the town and emptied taverns. One chronicler described men going 'wetshod in wine'.

Dynastic War Begins

Parliament met at Coventry in the aftermath at a session later dubbed The Parliament of Devils. York, his sons, Salisbury, Warwick and others were attainted and found guilty of treason. This left them stripped of all their lands and titles and left with nothing to hand to the next generation. For a noble family, it was a dynastic death. The events of autumn 1458 had driven an argument over who best to advise a weak king into a dynastic struggle for the Crown of England. In their fear, Henry and Margaret had pushed York until he had nothing left to lose and perhaps felt that he had no option remaining but to take the ultimate step. They were in danger of repeating the difficulties between Richard II and Henry IV.

Henry ordered a fleet assembled on the south coast to dislodge the Yorkist lords at Calais. Warwick simply sailed across the Channel and stole the ships, as well as taking Richard Woodville and his son Anthony captive. Salisbury, Warwick and Edward hurled abuse at their prisoners. Given that Edward would later marry Richard Woodville's daughter, it was an awkward first meeting with his future father-in-law and brother-in-law. In June 1460, the three Yorkist leaders crossed the Channel to Sandwich. Marching on London, Salisbury laid siege to the Tower, held once again by Lord Scales as it had been during Cade's Rebellion.

Lord Scales reacted to the new threat by unleashing wildfire on the mob below. A sticky substance similar to napalm, it burned all it came into contact with and couldn't be extinguished with water, as those who flung themselves into the Thames discovered. The brutal tactics earned Scales, and the royal cause, the hatred of Londoners. Leaving Salisbury to crack the Tower, Warwick and Edward marched north, searching for Henry VI. They found him and an army at Northampton on 10 July. Both sides were suffering in the torrential rain as a parlay began. As a mark of the escalating conflict, this was the last time a parlay would occur before a battle on English soil. When battle commenced, the royal army was nestled in a bend in a river and protected in front by defences they had prepared. The first problem came when their gunpowder weapons were rendered useless by the weather.

As the Yorkist forces approached, Lord Grey, on the left flank of the royal army, laid down his weapons and allowed Edward's men to pass through the defences. He had made contact before the battle and offered to change sides, a common occurrence during the Wars of the Roses. Once the Yorkists were inside the defences, the royal force had little hope. The Duke of Buckingham was killed along with the Earl of Shrewsbury and a brother of the Earl of Northumberland. Henry was left behind as his men fled and Warwick and Edward took him into custody.

It took three months for York to return from Ireland, a delay that suggests he was still uncertain. On 10 October 1460, he arrived at a packed Westminster Hall, climbed the steps to the dais, and laid his hand on the empty throne. The meaning was clear to all present. York was claiming Henry's throne. He was greeted with complete silence. No one knew what to do or say. When the Chancellor asked York if he wished to see the king, the embarrassed duke flew into a rage, saying Henry ought to come and see him instead.

LISTEN TO THE
PODCAST

Dynastic Clashes in
the Wars of the Roses

Parliament met in a charged environment to debate the competing claims. York asserted that descent from Edward III's second son defeated Henry's descent from the third son and that the Mortimer line had always been the rightful one. York answered all of the criticisms of his claim with ease. When representatives of Parliament visited Henry to ask him to provide a defence of his Crown, he declined and asked them to do it for him. Unable to defeat York's logic and with Henry unwilling to oppose the duke, Parliament finally agreed that York held the superior claim. On 25 October 1460, the Act of Accord was passed. The compromise was that Henry should remain king for the rest of his life. York would be appointed his heir, and the Crown would pass to York and his heirs on Henry's death. In the meantime, York would take control of the government and be given an income as heir to the throne. The compromise suggests York was not as driven by ambition for the Crown as many believed.

Margaret of Anjou was incensed by the settlement. She heard of the news while in Wales with her son, Prince Edward. They travelled to Scotland and agreed to hand over the strategic border town of Berwick in return for Scottish support. With no money, Margaret promised the army pay in whatever they could loot as they moved south. When news of the army crossing the border reached London, York and Salisbury, with York's second son Edmund, raised a force and moved north. They stopped at Sandal Castle near Wakefield to await reinforcements from York's son Edward.

When other troops arrived before Edward, York believed he had the numbers, and launched an attack on 30 December 1460. It was a trap. As soon as he was outside the castle walls, the new recruits turned on him. The Battle of Wakefield saw York killed and his son Edmund hunted down by Lord Clifford in revenge for his father's death. Salisbury was captured but dragged out of prison by a mob the next day and beheaded. All three heads were spiked on Micklegate Bar, one of the gates into the city of York. A paper crown was fixed to York's head to mock his royal pretensions. The Wars of the Roses had reached new levels of brutality.

The fight for the throne had no name during the 15th century. The early Tudor government adopted the white and red rose combined as a badge and referred to rose motifs. The House of York did use a white rose as one of its emblems, but the red rose was never a recognised badge of the House of Lancaster. The conflict is sometimes referred to as the Cousins' War due to the closely related nature of all those involved. The term Wars of the Roses was first coined by Sir Walter Scott in his novel *Anne of Geierstein* in 1829, and the first use of the term the Cousins' War appeared in the second half of the twentieth century.

Edward had been delayed in the Marches as a Lancastrian army led by Jasper Tudor, Earl of Pembroke marched out of Wales. Edward confronted them at the Battle of Mortimer's Cross on 2 February 1461. Before the engagement, a parhelion appeared in the sky. Also known as a sun dog, this is the refraction of ice crystals in the sunlight, and it made it look as though there were three suns in the sky. Edward's men feared it was a bad omen, but Edward told them it meant the Holy Trinity – Father, Son and Holy Ghost – were watching over them. The Yorkists went on to win a crushing victory. Jasper escaped, but his father, Owen Tudor, widower of Catherine of Valois, was caught and executed at Hereford, where a local lady cared for his severed head for days, brushing his hair and washing his face.

Warwick positioned himself at St Albans to block Margaret's army from the north from reaching London. On 17 February 1461, Warwick was soundly defeated at the Second Battle of St Albans. Margaret pushed on south to try to recover her husband from the capital. The Lancastrian army, with its Scottish contingent, was denied entry into a nervous London and was forced to turn back north. When Edward and Warwick arrived in the capital, Edward was proclaimed king. In legal terms the attack on York, the heir to the throne, was treason. It was decided that the Act of Accord had been breached. A delegation of Lords and Londoners, tired of Henry's ineffectual rule, asked Edward to take the throne on 4 March 1461, aged 18. He accepted, but refused to be crowned while an enemy army was in the fields. As he and Warwick gathered a fresh army to move north, the stage was set for an apocalyptic confrontation.

England's Apocalypse

At the Battle of Towton on Palm Sunday, 29 March 1461, two vast armies met in swirling wind and snow. Local and national feuds were settled in brutal fashion. Contemporary estimates, almost certainly vastly inflated, give around 100,000 men in the field, with 28,000 dead. It was certainly the bloodiest battle on English soil, exceeding the first day of the Battle of the Somme in

World War One if the figures are correct. The battle began with an archery duel. The wind was behind the Yorkists, whose arrows hit home relentlessly as the Lancastrians' efforts fell short. When they had run out of ammunition, the Yorkist archers stepped forward and collected the Lancastrian arrows to shoot back. The battle was a close-run affair for a long time. Eventually, the Duke of Norfolk arrived late to reinforce the Yorkist side, and the Lancastrian force broke and fled, many pursued and cut down or drowned in the swollen waterways around them.

Edward returned to London for his coronation on 28 June 1461. It took a long time to settle the north. Somerset, the Lancastrian commander, had escaped, and Henry VI was still at large. There were now two kings and only one Crown. Somerset was briefly reconciled with Edward but soon slipped back into the Lancastrian camp. On 25 April 1464, he led an ambush on an escort heading north to collect Scottish ambassadors but was roundly beaten at the Battle of Hedgeley Moor. He tried again as they returned south on 15 May, but was captured at the Battle of Hexham and executed. Henry was caught soon afterwards and taken to London to be placed in the Tower. All seemed settled for Edward IV, the first Yorkist King of England.

As the 1460s progressed, Edward became increasingly distanced from his powerful and influential cousin Warwick. Having helped Edward to the throne, Warwick perhaps hoped for greater rewards, particularly a dukedom, but instead, as Edward grew more confident, he relied less and less on his cousin. The distance between them is frequently blamed on Edward's marriage. In 1464, while Warwick was finalising details of a prestigious foreign match for Edward, the king announced that he was already married. He had secretly wed the widow of a Lancastrian knight. Elizabeth Woodville was the oldest child of Richard Woodville and Jacquetta of Luxembourg. Her mother's lineage meant she was not a commoner, but neither was this an effective use of one of a medieval king's most potent diplomatic weapons: his marriage.

Elizabeth brought with her six sisters and five brothers, who quickly cornered the marriage market. Perhaps the most scandalous of the matches came when John, aged 19, married the 65-year-old Dowager Duchess of Norfolk. All of this made the Woodville family unpopular, particularly with the nobility, who saw opportunity being hoovered up. Warwick, with two daughters and no son, had relied on strong marriages to protect his family's future. Suddenly, there were none left.

Contemporary writers are clear that the real cause of the rift between Edward and Warwick was foreign policy. Edward favoured an alliance with Burgundy to facilitate trade and perhaps renew opportunities to attack France. Warwick wanted a French alliance, not least because he harboured a deep personal hatred of the Duke of Burgundy's son and heir, Charles. When Edward settled on Burgundy and married his sister Margaret to Charles when he succeeded his father, the matter was settled, and Warwick slipped into rebellion. The earl courted Edward's brother George, Duke of Clarence, who was heir presumptive to Edward's throne. George joined the rebellion with the promise that he would replace Edward as king. Their youngest brother, Richard, Duke of Gloucester, remained loyal to Edward throughout.

In July 1469, the Battle of Edgcote saw a rebel army supporting Warwick defeat one moving towards the Midlands to support Edward. The king was taken captive, and Warwick tried to rule in his name. Finding it impossible to raise an army without a king as Scotland threatened the northern border, Warwick released Edward, and there was a show of reconciliation. By March 1470, the rebellion was under way again. Edward met a rebel army at the Battle of Losecoat Field, so named because he routed his enemies, who shed their livery coats as they fled to avoid being identified as rebels and so they could run away faster. Warwick was driven into exile and ended up at the French court.

Here, Louis XI, known as the Universal Spider for the webs of intrigue he spun, brought Warwick before Margaret of Anjou, Henry VI's queen. He convinced them both that they were each other's best hope of a return to power. The enemies formed a new alliance after Margaret kept Warwick on his knees before her for more than a quarter of an hour. Henry VI would be restored. Warwick's daughter Anne would marry Margaret's son Prince Edward. George, who was married to Warwick's other daughter Isabel, would be heir to the Lancastrian line if it failed. He had been bumped right down the line of succession.

The Readeption of Henry VI

Warwick invaded England and caught Edward off-guard. The king was forced to sail into exile in Burgundy on 2 October 1470. Henry VI was wheeled out of the Tower. He was bedraggled and poorly cared for, which inspired little enthusiasm among the people. Warwick acted as effective regent until Prince Edward could cross from France. It is this period of aiding Edward IV's rise, his deposition, and Henry's reinstatement that led to Warwick's epithet of the Kingmaker. Parliament was summoned, though the records of the session would later be destroyed. The return to the throne of a deposed king required a name. No one knew what to call it, so they invented a word: readeption.

Edward was not idle in Burgundy. He prepared to retake his kingdom, and his opportunity came when France declared war on the duchy. The Burgundian Duke Charles, known as the Bold, backed Edward's return to England to prevent Warwick from joining Louis's attack. Blown off course by a storm, Edward landed at Ravenspur in Yorkshire, the same port that Henry IV had arrived at in 1399 when he deposed Richard II, with his brother Gloucester and a small force. Initially, Edward claimed he no longer wanted the Crown, only the return of the Duchy of York. Once he reached the Midlands, he shed the pretence. George rejoined his two brothers; the chronicles make it clear that their mother and sisters had been working to bring about a reconciliation between them.

On 14 April 1470, Edward met Warwick's army on a foggy morning at the Battle of Barnet. The poor visibility caused the armies to line up off-centre. The unbalanced fight eventually went Edward's way, with Warwick and his brother both killed in the retreat. After returning to London, Edward retrieved his family from sanctuary at Westminster to discover he had a new son and heir, born while he was in exile and named Edward. When news arrived that Margaret and her son had landed on the southwest coast on the same day as Barnet, Edward led an army out of the capital, heading west. After days of marching long distances in baking, dry weather, the Yorkists met the Lancastrian army at Tewkesbury, where they were trying to cross the River Severn to join Welsh allies.

On 4 May 1471, the two armies engaged. It was another close-run thing for a while, but Edward was again victorious. The Lancastrian Prince of Wales was killed, probably in the fighting, but perhaps afterwards. Several Lancastrian soldiers and their surviving leaders made it into Tewkesbury Abbey, but Edward had them dragged out and executed. Among them was Edmund Beaufort, Duke of Somerset, the last of the legitimate male line of the family. As a form of apology to the abbey, Edward had it redecorated but used Yorkist colours and emblems, which can still be seen today. The Princes of Wales was buried within the abbey, beneath the resplendent Yorkist symbols.

It is striking that all of Edward's victories during the Wars of the Roses were accompanied by a weather phenomenon of some kind, from a parhelion to rain, to snow, to fog, to extreme heat.

With Henry's heir dead and Margaret captured, Edward returned to London. On the day he entered the capital, it was announced that Henry VI had died in the Tower 'of pure melancholy' upon hearing the news. It has widely been believed since that he was murdered on Edward's instructions.

Having regained his Crown, Edward turned his attention to France, which had facilitated the readeption. In 1475, he launched a huge invasion of Louis's kingdom, claiming the French Crown. Edward's ally, the Duke of Burgundy, failed to support the invasion. Louis, who knew his enemies well, offered Edward huge sums of money to leave France. Edward accepted and withdrew, and from then on received an annual pension from Louis that Edward framed as a tribute.

George was never satisfied with his position. Having been forgiven for previous treachery, in 1477 he finally went too far. George was accused of taking royal authority into his own hands when he had one of his wife's ladies-in-waiting executed. He believed the lady had poisoned Isabel, causing her death shortly after childbirth. Given later events, George may have threatened to reveal dangerous information about Edward's marriage. His attainder stated that he was a threat to the queen and her children. George was executed on Edward's order. Although the method of the execution is not recorded, tradition claims he was drowned in a vat of malmsey wine.

In 1482, Edward's brother Richard led a campaign into Scotland, holding Edinburgh for several days. Trouble with Scotland was often a prelude to problems with France, and now Louis suddenly stopped paying Edward's pension. Edward had planned to lead the Scottish campaign himself but wrote to the Pope to explain that what he described as threats in the south, undoubtedly the French, prevented him from going north. Richard was given command instead. The plan was to replace King James III with his brother, the Duke of Albany. As the English approached, the Scots lords took the unpopular James into custody and locked him in Edinburgh Castle. Albany abandoned his English allies. When Richard arrived in the capital, he found no enemy to fight and no king to negotiate with. After several days of talks with the city authorities, Richard secured some promises and concessions from them and marched back south. He oversaw the capture of Berwick. This would be the last time it changed hands.

A Year of Three Kings

As French ships began aggressive moves in the Channel, Edward IV unexpectedly died after a short illness, in early April 1483. Sources suggest he caught a chill while fishing, though his true cause of death is unclear. The date is traditionally given as 9 April, but a notice of his passing the previous day arrived in York on 7 April. He may have died a few days earlier, and it had been kept secret because of the problems that would follow. He was 40 years old and left behind a 12-year-old heir, who was proclaimed King Edward V. Edward was considered an immensely likeable man with the common touch. He had been the glue that had held England together in the wake of the end of Lancastrian rule. Without him, there was the threat of a return to factions.

Over the following weeks, tensions mounted in London between the Woodville family and Lord Hastings, Edward's closest friend, who was engaged in a long-running feud with the queen's family. Both sides were reported putting armed men into the streets of London as they vied for power. By a late codicil added to Edward's will, Richard, Duke of Gloucester was appointed Protector, as his father had been. He left the north with warning from Hastings of what the Woodvilles were up to ringing in his ears. He met the new king at Stony Stratford, where he claimed to have exposed a Woodville plot on Richard's life. He arrested several men, took custody of young Edward, travelled on to London and set about organising the coronation of his nephew.

The events of the summer of 1483 are complex. A story would emerge that Edward IV had married Elizabeth Woodville bigamously. This may have been the revelation George had threatened to make in 1477. Evidence of bigamy was produced, examined and accepted, though some have claimed that it was all a fabrication. Once accepted as proven, the bigamy made Edward's children illegitimate. They were set aside, and their uncle was offered the Crown, becoming King Richard III on 26 June 1483. The actions and motives of key players during that period, from Hastings to Richard, from Buckingham to Queen Elizabeth, are hotly debated, and the lack of evidence requires some subjective judgement. Was Richard an ambitious monster who stole the Crown or the unexpecting recipient of an unlooked-for position?

In October 1483, Richard faced a rebellion led by his erstwhile ally Henry Stafford, Duke of Buckingham, who, as a descendant of Edward III, made his own bid for the throne. Torrential rain caused the River Severn to swell and hamper the revolt, continuing the House of York's fortuitous relationship with the weather. The majority of the rebels were shire gentry in the southeast. As with so much around the story of Richard III, why they rose is unclear and contentious. Was Richard a tyrant who might have murdered his nephews, the Princes in the Tower, or did his efforts to drive out corruption hurt the pockets of the layer of society who tried to remove him?

LISTEN TO THE
PODCAST

End of the Wars
of the Roses

Rise of the Tudors

A new rival emerged in exile. Henry Tudor was the son of Lady Margaret Beaufort from her brief marriage to Edmund Tudor, Henry VI's half-brother. Edmund had died before Henry was born in 1457, and Henry had been taken to Brittany by his uncle Jasper Tudor in 1471 when the Lancastrian readeption collapsed. The Beaufort line gave Henry a tenuous link to the throne. He appealed to those disaffected with Richard III because his lack of experience of England made him appear pliable. This support was bolstered when Henry Tudor pledged to marry Edward IV's oldest daughter, Elizabeth of York. Louis XI died within weeks of Edward IV. Louis's heir, Charles VIII, was 13 years old, so France now faced the troubles of a minority that England had avoided. Richard, who had opposed Edward's peace with France in 1475, was operating a much more aggressive foreign policy that might have seen the reignition of the Hundred Years' War.

In 1485, with French backing and English exiles, Henry Tudor set sail to claim the Crown of England. He landed at Mill Bay in southwest Wales and played up his Welsh heritage as he gathered support on his march. Heading north, he reached Machynlleth, then cut east across Wales to Shrewsbury. Around this time, Henry met with his stepfather, Thomas, Lord Stanley, Lady Margaret Beaufort's fourth husband. Stanley seems to have pledged his support to his stepson and to Richard III at the same time. Henry picked up the old Roman road of Watling Street, now the A5, that headed straight for London. Richard, who had been making military preparations at Nottingham in the kingdom's centre, moved to Leicester, then to Market Bosworth to cut off Tudor's path to the capital.

At the Battle of Bosworth on 22 August 1485, Henry Tudor's unlikely band faced the royal army of Richard III. John Howard,

Duke of Norfolk led Richard's vanguard against the Earl of Oxford. Norfolk would be killed in the fighting. Richard led a thunderous cavalry charge across the field to kill Henry Tudor and end the fight. The haste was caused by the presence of the Stanley army, led by Thomas's brother Sir William. They sat to one side, no one sure where they would strike. Richard may have hoped that getting to Tudor quickly would prevent the Stanley force from being forced to make a choice.

Richard came close, unhorsing a 6'7" knight and killing Tudor's standard-bearer, whose role was to stand at his leader's side. As Richard's men began to fall, William Stanley led his forces into the fray, decisively turning the battle in Henry Tudor's favour.

Richard made a brave last stand. Even hostile chroniclers praised his courage and tenacity. One Tudor writer explained that he died 'fighting in the thickest press of his enemies'. When Richard fell, William Stanley found the crown the king had worn on his helmet in imitation of Henry V at Agincourt. Passing it to Henry Tudor, he made a new king, and a new dynasty.

The Battle of Bosworth became a defining moment. Not just the end of 30 years of civil strife but of the entire medieval period. It ended 331 years of Plantagenet rule, from Henry II to Richard II, and ushered in the Tudor dynasty. A great deal changed, but the medieval period did not end with the strike of a single blow on one day. Henry VII would be keen to paint his reign as a new beginning, but it was markedly medieval as he initially employed Edward IV's former men.

England had been forged into a new, distinct nation in the four centuries since Hastings. The process was not ended at Bosworth.

Conclusion

While England was enwrapped in dynastic conflict and invading France, a quiet revolution was taking place. In 1440, Johannes Gutenberg invented the first moveable type printing press in Germany. By 1476, it had found its way into a Westminster workshop set up by William Caxton. Prior to the printing press's invention, information moved painfully slowly. Books were expensive and laborious to produce, with church clerics often writing out copies, which limited the spread of information and ideas. The printing press allowed copies of text to be reproduced quickly. Like the Internet 500 years later, the invention would define the century that followed. While the Battle of Bosworth is often recognised as the end-point of medieval England, new technology across Europe was also ushering in a new era. Maritime navigation leaped forward, and Christopher Columbus reached the Americas just seven years into Henry VII's reign. The Catholic Church would soon face its greatest challenge since its creation.

There is a temptation to see the medieval period as a stagnant moment in history when little really changed in 1,000 years. This book, covering only the second half of that millennium, recounts spectacular changes in England, beginning with a military and cultural conquest. Under the Normans, England was once again part of a collection of lands, as it had been briefly under Danish rule. The kingdom also became more politically connected to the continent than it had been since the Roman occupation; this was intensified by Henry II's Angevin Empire. Institutions of government had been created to deal with absentee monarchs and sprawling responsibilities. The Exchequer and the Chancery Office created an early civil service to support the Crown, allowing England to function in the absence of a monarch.

The slow integration of Magna Carta, its progress from a failed revolt to a constitutional cornerstone, began the process of examining and regularising the Crown's relationship with the political body of the realm. The emergence within decades of Parliament as a body that balanced that relationship, initially by granting taxation in return for reform, laid broad foundations upon which would be built the increasingly confident assertion of parliamentary authority and power. By the 14th century, it was the forum in which monarchs could be legally deposed and replaced, a power that went beyond that of the Anglo-Saxon Witenagemot. By the 15th century, the approval of Parliament was considered vital in the acceptance of a new king, restoring at least the veneer of the elective element of Anglo-Saxon kingship. There was a departure from the absolutist monarchy that grew in France.

The unexpected consequence of the devastation of the Black Death was the creation of ambition for a better life that felt within reach. The government reacted by snatching that opportunity away. The Peasants' Revolt of 1381 was a reaction to the withdrawal of that hope. Although the lower classes were crushed, they had come tantalisingly close to what they wanted. Violent protest had driven home to the minority elite the dangers of squeezing those beneath them too hard. More balance was built in, even if it still favoured those at the top.

This new ambition would feed innovation. The restraints still placed on the lower classes made it slower than it might otherwise have been. The emergence in society of the merchant class, something like a middle class, helped draw money and opportunity down to a wider group than before. From the wool merchant Laurence of Ludlow building himself Stokesay Castle in the 13th century to Caxton investing in new technology to create a market for books in which he could profit, opportunity was there. The pursuit of this drove exploration. It was not the noble elite who sailed to Africa in search of new commodities and markets, or to the New World in 1492. Innovation came from the people, because those already at the top had no interest in change. Stagnation was in their interests.

Exploration and discovery in turn shifted the balance of power in medieval Europe. During the 15th century, the Great Bullion Famine had seen a shortage of gold and silver that was relieved by the discovery of the New World. Access to this fresh supply, and the other commercial and political opportunities provided by exploration, were controlled by Spain and Portugal. France had been at the core of Europe for so long that, to many in the Near East, all Europeans were Franks. England had gone from being the most significant continental power under Henry II to one consumed by a civil war that controlled nothing beyond Calais. The great rivalry between England and France that dominated the thoughts of both prevented a focus on broader issues and opportunities. Still, that conflict went a long way to defining both nations in terms of their international outlook and their internal concerns.

Religious reform was a central concern during the medieval period that led directly to the Protestant Reformation of the 16th century. Martin Luther was viewed as the successor to Jan Hus, the Czech reformer burned at the stake in 1415, as England embarked on the Agincourt campaign. Hus was heavily influenced by John Wycliffe, whose views appear very similar to Protestantism. Hussites and Lollards were part of the journey to Martin Luther's Ninety-five Theses. Protestantism did not erupt into being in 1517, it was a consequence of a long-existing desire for reform that had its roots in medieval England. What had changed was the increased access to ideas and the ability to spread them brought by the printing press.

The early deconstruction of absolute monarchy in England through a set of robust and confident institutions, led by Parliament, is perhaps the single most important factor in the endurance of the British monarchy as other European Crowns fell away. There was always a balance, it is only the precise point of the fulcrum that has moved, adapting with time and a changing world. England toyed with republicanism before other nations did but ultimately decided against it in a 17th-century experiment, the Commonwealth, yet to be repeated. This early decision and the medieval foundational structures of government positioned Great Britain to launch the Industrial Revolution just as the French Revolution took place.

The move between historical epochs was often a result of a combination of factors and took time to effect change. Sir Thomas More (1478–1535) lived through the transition from Medieval into Early Modern. The transitional nature, and the awareness of those living through it of the sense of change, can be seen in two of his most famous works. Begun in the 1510s, *The History of King Richard the Third* is a piece of medieval litera-ture. It uses history as allegory for the delivery of contemporary political messages. It does not seek to deliver historical truths or accuracy but to use the lessons of history to try to direct the actions of politicians of the day. It is an allegorical warning to the young Henry VIII of the dangers of tyranny. Alongside this, More wrote *Utopia*, in which his narrator explores the idea of a perfect island society. This ideal adopts many principles More was known to oppose – married clergy, no private property, etc. It is a new way of writing, in which there is no allusion to reality. It is fiction that is self-aware of its status as such. More's parallel work in these two styles mirrors the change he saw in the world around him. A new age was being born, but the labour was long. Ultimately, More never completed *The History of King Richard the Third*, but did finish and publish *Utopia*. He recognised the need to set down the old ways and embrace the new, but the change was creeping, not abrupt.

The medieval world did not end with the Battle of Bosworth on 22 August 1485. In England, the government of Henry VII, the first Tudor, was strikingly Yorkist in nature. Across Europe a variety of movements, from religious reform to a renaissance in art and architecture, melted and melded with exploration and discovery to create a new horizon. As the Internet defines how the world develops today, so did the printing press half a millennium ago. We are not separated from the medieval world.

Acknowledgements

A book is always the sum of the work of many more people than those that appear on the cover. History Hit's team, including Amy Irvine, Kyle Hoekstra, Lily Johnson and Dan Snow, provided invaluable support in making sure this book happened. Thank you also to Hodder, and particularly to Rupert Lancaster and Lucy Buxton for all their help in getting this to publication, and to Briony Hartley at Goldust Design, for wrangling it into a format that makes it look the part.

There are numerous QR codes throughout this book, most of which link to selected episodes of *Gone Medieval* that complement and expand on the text. *Gone Medieval* is an absolute pleasure to work on, thanks to the brilliant team behind every episode at History Hit, which includes Steve Lanham, Elena Guthrie, Rob Weinberg, Joseph Knight and Ella Blaxill.

The wonderful guests we have on *Gone Medieval* offer a wide range of views on varied topics across the period, all of which come together to paint vivid pictures of possibly the most important and interesting millennium in human history. You can hear many of those guests by following the QR codes in this book, but there is also a growing back catalogue of episodes on all aspects and regions of the medieval world. I learn something from every episode I have the pleasure of taking part in – or listening to, in the case of the episodes led by my brilliant co-host Dr Eleanor Janega. That, in turn, adds to my perception and understanding of medieval England and has contributed to the presentation of its history in this book.

Finally, I would like to offer a special acknowledgement and thank you to James Carson for giving me the role at History Hit, which has genuinely been a dream come true. During his tenure, James expertly drove History Hit forward and explored new opportunities with flair, including creating books, and I remain eternally grateful for the opportunities he gave me.

Any errors or omissions within these pages are entirely mine.

Picture Acknowledgements

© Alamy Photo: Pages iii, x, 10, 17, 22, 33, 36, 39, 42, 53, 54, 61, 63, 67, 72, 75, 76, 78, 81, 90, 96, 107, 110, 133, 140, 145, 148, 152, 155, 160, 164, 171, 174, 179, 181, 186, 200, 208, 218, 223, 226, 235, 241, 249, 252, 258, 272

© Bridgeman Images: Pages 24, 27, 97, 109, 112, 130, 138, 150, 202, 206, 221, 228, 244, 267, 275, 277

© Shutterstock.com: Pages 88, 92, 105, 121, 125, 195

© Herzog August Bibliothek Wolfenbuettel: Cod. Guelf. 105 Noviss. 2°, fol. 171v: Page 50

© Moment @ Getty Images: Page 68

© Hulton Archive @ Getty Images: Pages 116, 190

© Universal History Archive @ Getty Images: Page 142

© Archive Photos @ Getty Images: Page 215

Maps: © Joanna Boyle

Index